INTERNATIONAL MORALITY

IS VOLUME

106

OF THE

Twentieth Century Encyclopedia of Catholicism

UNDER SECTION

IX

THE CHURCH AND THE MODERN WORLD

IT IS ALSO THE

105TH

VOLUME IN ORDER OF PUBLICATION

Edited by HENRI DANIEL-ROPS of the Académie Française

INTERNATIONAL
MORALITY

By *ALFRED DE SORAS, S.J.*

Translated from the French by S. J. Tester

19527

HAWTHORN BOOKS · PUBLISHERS · *New York*

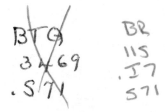

First Edition, August, 1963

NIHIL OBSTAT

Joannes M. T. Barton, S.T.D., L.S.S.

   Censor Deputatus

IMPRIMATUR

Georgius L. Craven

   Episcopus Sebastopolis, Vic. Cap.

Westmonasterii, die XV MARTII MCMLXIII

H-9541

CONTENTS

CHAPTER I

THE NATURE AND SUBJECTS OF INTERNATIONAL MORALITY

WHAT DOES INTERNATIONAL MORALITY MEAN?

Although the expression "international morality" is established in usage, it is certainly not entirely felicitous: it should mean, taken strictly literally, "the morality of relations between nations". Now not only has the idea of a "nation" undergone an extremely complex process of historical evolution, but in the course of that evolution its content has varied and is still changing. Despite the analyses of contemporary historians, sociologists, lawyers and economists, that idea still resists exact definition. It is difficult to be precise about it while recognizing its diverse historical, sociological and economic aspects; for in our everyday speech we use the word "nation" in an unreflecting and over-simplified way as if we could include all this diversity easily and without inaccuracy under the same "blanket" term.

We might suggest, following some recent views in sociology, that a nation is a limited ethnic unit more or less spontaneously animated by a desire to live as a community in order to pursue common aims. If this is right, the sociological phenomenon of nationhood would seem to be dependent not only on *objective facts* (the general conditions for the historical birth and growth of a national group, conditions of geographical place, of soil, of climate, of language, of economy, of customs and institutions, and so on), but also, and especially, on *subjective factors* which are more or less spontaneous (the desire to live together, mutual agreement on the ideas of values and of the common ends to be pursued, etc.), and which, moreover, are manifested externally and publicly in certain inevitable ways. It is at the same time clear that the sociological phenomenon of nationhood is capable of embracing countless degrees of maturity and stability. History tells us as much. There are nations such as those of western Europe, fully established after long centuries of common history and culture. But there are also the nations now coming into being, in which the desire to live as a community has remained more instinctive and emotional than reflective and rational, and in which the values to be commonly pursued are conceived, if not by the educated minorities, at least by the great majority of the people, in a very confused way. Nationhood as it actually is thus presents the appearance of being inchoate, limited, sometimes precarious, and even perhaps provisional.

All the same, the national desire to live as a community, in proportion as it achieves or preserves stability, tends spontaneously, as it were, to its logical limit, to find its adequate legal expression in a *nation-State* more or less similar to the great European States, which are in fact the perfect types of nation-States. Yet, because of certain particular historical facts, this natural and spontaneous tendency has not always been able to arrive at that end. There are nations, such as the Baltic nations today, which are not, or are no longer, States.

Because the idea of a "nation" is to some extent affected by such uncertainties, inexactitude, historical forces and interrupted developments, it is often difficult or even impossible to state with real precision what "moral subjects" are covered by an international morality thought of as a "morality of relations between nations".[1]

Now we cannot enter upon the consideration of such problems here; they are very difficult, and in any case too complex and diversified to be sorted out and solved within the compass of this book. We shall therefore deliberately restrict the idea of international morality to that of a morality of the relations between States, and even *between contemporary States.*[2] In other words, international morality will be considered in this book as *that branch of ethics which should furnish the States of today with the rules of conduct which should govern their relations.*[3] It may be that

---

[1] This difficulty was shown in very strong relief at the time of the Treaty of Versailles, when the attempt was made to apply too strictly the "principle of sovereign States" so dear to Wilson. Moreover, the presence of minorities within certain established States and the problems thus generated show that the coincidence of the nation-community and the State-community is not always ideal.

[2] We shall limit ourselves to *contemporary* States. Obviously, a textbook of *International Morality* could and should consider the behaviour of the States of the past, which were different in their structure and their life from those of today; but such consideration of what ought to have been the conduct of States in earlier historical situations is too complicated to be undertaken in a few pages, and is besides only of theoretical interest. We shall therefore confine ourselves to the present.

[3] A similar narrowing of the sense of the word *international* is to be seen in the practice of modern Public International Law, which is applied to *States* or *organizations created by pacts and conventions between States.* In spite of its title, the United Nations Charter itself speaks in its articles only of *member-States* (e.g., Art. 2, 1.6; Art. 3, etc.). Pius XII also, who in his allocutions and encyclicals frequently referred to international morality, himself took it to refer to the morality governing the States of today (e.g., the encyclical *Summi Pontificatus* and the Christmas messages of 1941 and 1942, etc.). Since the Renaissance the traditional *ius gentium* (literally "the law of peoples") has been increasingly formulated in terms of the rights and duties of States.

the correct title for this book should be "Contemporary Inter-State Morality".

There are today, of course, besides the nation-States—and the encouraging nature of this fact will be stressed later on—a good number of international organizations; and it must be admitted that international morality is concerned not only with the conduct of States among themselves, but also with the conduct proper to such international organizations.[4]

WHAT ARE THE CONCRETE MORAL SUBJECTS DIRECTLY AFFECTED BY INTERNATIONAL MORALITY?

International morality being so defined, the question arises, what exactly are the concrete moral subjects the theorists have in mind in formulating it? Some elucidation of this question is needed.

We may say that a State, in the modern sense of the term,[5] is a group of men living in a determinate territory, constituting an organized body politic under a sovereign authority which is charged with achieving the common

[4] It is difficult to define the dividing line between the two sets of subjects of international morality in the present state of the world. In fact, the international organizations of today are generally organizations defined and established by pacts and conventions made between States and subject to revision. The United Nations Organization itself is not, in the full and strict meaning of the words, a supra-State or supra-national organization. Its decisions and acts are thus *de facto* the results, to a large extent, of decisions taken and actions adopted by the member-States within the U.N.O. It thus seems that in international society as it is today, the theory of international morality must be concerned in the first instance with States. It would certainly be different if there were a world authority the policies of which were not determined by the policies of particular States. Perhaps it is even now different, if we can allow that the existence of present-day international organizations, although it is in each case dependent on agreement between the member States, is nevertheless an independent existence.

[5] Cf. J. L. Brierly, *The Law of Nations*, 5th edn, Oxford, 1955, p. 118, and the Earl of Birkenhead, *International Law*, 6th edn by R. Moelwyn-Hughes, Dent, 1927, p. 31.

good of the said group by the creation and effective administration of public services in accordance with the principles of an established rule of law.

Within the framework of this general idea there is room for various *forms of State*: single or independent States, such as Great Britain, France, Spain, etc.; federal States, such as the U.S.A., Australia, Canada, etc. Within the field even of single, independent States, the form of government, the seat of power, can vary infinitely, being democratic or dictatorial, under a president or a monarch or a legislative assembly, and so on. But in all there is one common feature: in every case, there is at the head of the State an authority broadly responsible for political decisions. The life of a State is very largely ruled by the decisions of its government.

It therefore follows that international morality is directly concerned with governments. Now governments are merely "moral persons" actually composed of governors (heads of State, ministers, deputies, senators, etc.). Fundamentally, then, international morality has to form and influence the moral conscience of these politicians who, in their various ways, form governments.

For similar reasons—for whatever their form, international organizations are also actually made up of human persons—international morality should apply directly to the consciences of the politicians who exercise some function in such organizations.

WHAT ARE THE MORAL SUBJECTS TO WHICH INTERNATIONAL MORALITY INDIRECTLY APPLIES?

It would be a mistake to imagine that the application of international morality is restricted to governors and international officials alone. Many private citizens, in fact, influence the behaviour of such governors and officials, and do so in many ways. Firstly, whatever the established régime, the policies of statesmen are, today at least, affected by general public opinion. Again, in contemporary democratic States, the people, through elections and systems of representation in parliaments and assemblies, have some control over the decisions of their governors. Thirdly, the lawyers have a particularly important influence, for they formulate or interpret the rules of law which at any given time the governors must observe to establish such and such relations between their own State and others. So, little by little it is, at least indirectly, the moral conscience of all men, private and public, lawyers and non-lawyers, which international morality must form and influence in order to give moral rightness to the whole of international life. We can say, if we like, that indirectly the subjects of international morality are all men in the world.

This has been fully realized by the Catholic Church, which has encouraged the creation and development of movements such as *Pax Christi*, which was established precisely to spread among the public at large the knowledge of a true international morality.

CHAPTER II

THE
AIMS OF CATHOLIC
INTERNATIONAL
MORALITY

The international morality set out here, as is only to be expected in a book in this series, is that inspired by Catholicism. Now in order to describe in a general way the fundamental aim of such a Catholic international morality, we must begin by analysing the conditions under which politicians ought to make their decisions if they want them to be truly reasonable and right.

The achievement of the correct solution of any political problem, whether international or not, requires that the politicians who are responsible for finding a concrete and effective solution should be careful to do three things: they should analyse as objectively and completely as possible the facts of the situation from which they start; they should take exact account of the technical means at their disposal (political, diplomatic, legal, economic, fiscal, etc.); and they should be clear, without bias, about the values to be preserved through whatever action is taken.

If this is so, the Catholic cannot claim, as a Catholic, any particular power to sum up adequately all the concrete facts of a given international situation. Nor can he claim any special power of discovering or making clear, without risk of error, the technical processes making possible an effective approach to the difficulties presented by the facts of the situation. But he can, because of that special vocation he believes to be theirs who have received the light of Christ, regard himself as having a right sense of the values which the actions of the experts in international politics should achieve and preserve.

In other words, the first object of international morality is to give to the minds and consciences of the men engaged in international politics the sense of the essential values which they should respect and pursue all through their concrete actions.

CATHOLIC INTERNATIONAL MORALITY AND "MORALITIES OF EXPEDIENCE"

One feature of Catholic international morality is extremely important: it tries to formulate its imperatives with reference to essential values. Right from the beginning it claims that an imperative cannot be begotten of the simple indicative statements given by the objective and scientific observation of given situations and facts. In this, Catholicism only claims to echo logic: at a time when objective science ruled the roost, Henri Poincaré pertinently observed that a norm of behaviour could never be the child of a factual report. A value-judgement can never validly be deduced from a judgement of fact, even if the latter is a collective judgement. The two kinds of statement are quite different.

In our own times, many men have found it difficult to hold on to this elementary logical position. But Catholic international morality should never yield on this point. Three times—in his allocution of April 24th, 1952; in an address of May 18th, 1952; and in a decree of the Holy Office of March 14th, 1956—Pius XII condemned the inconsistencies of recent systems of morality, both of groups and individuals, which are only "moralities of expedience". What Pius XII was saying was that one would have to dismiss all philosophical thinking to be able to pride oneself on having constructed systems of morality, for groups or individuals, which are only functions of simple, existential, factual judgements without any reference to universal and essential value-judgements. Such value-judgements overshadow the given existential or historical facts without being at the mercy of their contingence. These universal and essential value-judgements alone enable human freedom to create a properly moral system at the very heart of the varied and changing world of history.

From all this we can see how important it is that Catholics should work out an international morality. If the politician can expect the necessary analysis of the facts of any given situation and of the means at his disposal from the competent technical services, he needs the help of the moralist to reach the desired clarity and precision on the question of the values involved in the situation, even if he could, in simple cases at least, discover them on his own, provided his own conscience were strictly formed.

CATHOLIC INTERNATIONAL MORALITY AND PUBLIC INTERNATIONAL LAW

Now there are politicians who might claim to apprehend the meaning of these essential and absolute values merely by referring to the precepts of actual public international law. It is true that this law has been developed precisely in order to provide the politician with rules of conduct in international affairs, and that he is bound to consult the international lawyer. All the same, from the Catholic's point of view, such an *exclusive* reference to public international law would seem to be dubious on two counts.

First, do the present various codifications of public international law always reflect in their articles the essential and absolute values we have been speaking of? These codifications have arisen sometimes out of international treaties and agreements, sometimes out of established custom, and sometimes as the result of practical compromises between States. Now it cannot be proved, *a priori*, that these treaties, agreements, customs and compromises have always been inspired by a strict awareness of the absolute values which ought to be respected. Paul Reuter writes: "No one since the beginning of the nineteenth century has confused morality and law"[1], and Roscoe Pound: "The nineteenth-century jurist is zealous to point out that a legal right is not necessarily right, i.e., that it may or may not be accordant with the general feelings as to what ought to be. He is eager to show that one may have a legal claim that is morally wrong, and to refute the fallacious jingle that a legal right is not a right if it is not right."[2]

Such a separation of morality and positive law threatens more largely today because so many contemporary jurists, especially among the Anglo-Saxons, are empiricists: "Modern empiricists," writes Reuter, "voluntarily restrict themselves in order to be more scientifically rigorous. In their view, public international law is first and foremost a matter of observation: the jurist must accept the juridical rules of a society as they exist; his task therefore is not to deduce the rules from general principles, but on the contrary, as Grotius had already seen, to proceed from the particular rule to the general principle."[3] As can be seen,

[1] *International Institutions*, trans. J. M. Chapman, London, 1958, p. 66.
[2] *Law and Morals*, 2nd edn, University of North Carolina Press and Oxford University Press, 1926, pp. 34–5.
[3] *Op. cit.*, p. 65.

such legal positivism or empiricism, carried to its limits, would have to be included under "moralities of expedience", and as such would come under the fire of the same criticism of Pius XII in his first encyclical: "The ultimate and deepest reason for the evils in modern society we now deplore is the denial and rejection of a universal and absolute rule of morality either in the case of the individual or in that of society and international relations."

To be certain of the rightness of his policies, the politician must, then, always set the rules of public international law against the imperatives of international morality, and ask himself whether those rules do really confront him with true values.

The second point may be put in this way. Suppose, *per impossibile*, that positive law coincides completely with morality. Even so, we should have to agree that it could not include within the field of its established rules all the answers to the problems raised in actual international affairs. History, indeed, is always producing situations and problems which are unforeseeable and unforeseen, and necessarily so, which fall outside the "written law", and even, to a large extent, outside the extrapolations practised by the interpretations of jurisprudence. We have only to think, for example, of the problems posed by the present conquest of outer space and the invention of "missiles". In such new situations, where no recourse can be had to the "written law" of established rights, the politician, like Antigone, cannot but appeal to the "unwritten law" which establishes Right, graven in the hearts of men; it is precisely the business of international morality to give this unwritten law its permanent meaning. For a politician to try to carry out truly moral policies by referring only to established international law would be as senseless a gamble as for a husband, who wanted to spiritualize his conjugal life amid the changes of daily life, to try to find the rules of his human love only in the precepts of established family law. Just like man's love, his political life is a matter of "genius", of continuous "creation"; it must find its rightness in a spirit that no letter, no system of legal clauses could exhaust once for all. Appeal must be made to a spiritual discipline if politicians are not to be caught unprepared in questions of values, when they are faced with the new and particular cases with which history continually surprises them.

ONE INTERNATIONAL MORALITY AMONG MANY FORMS OF BEHAVIOUR

The Catholic moralist tends to create among men, through the system of ethics that he develops, a unanimous adherence to the fundamental value-judgements on which the details of all international morality rest. Does this mean that he tends at the same time to suppress all variety of properly political choices and legitimate, actual forms of conduct in any given international situation?

Many people think so. But this is a chimera men must guard against—particularly those who are among the too-committed champions of unanimity. In fact, as we have remarked above, for there to be complete agreement on some concrete action or political choice, there must be agreement on three things: on the values to be pursued; on the technical analysis of the situations presented by history; and on the precise means of setting about things as a result of that analysis and in view of those values. Now the moralist only claims—it is the only thing he could claim—to give all men the same understanding of true values. But in a new and complex international situation, the same doctrinal "orthodoxy" concerning values may legitimately allow, in many cases, a certain range of political and technical choices. When it is a matter of the technical analysis of an actual situation, men having the same ideals may differ; and choices may also be different when it is a matter of selecting the actual means of realizing a commonly understood and accepted ideal.

It can thus be understood that although the aim of Catholic international morality is to reach as close an agreement among men as is possible on value-judgements, it cannot aim at producing, nor can it automatically produce, a complete harmonization of actual forms of political action.

CHAPTER III

THE STRUCTURE OF CATHOLIC INTERNATIONAL MORALITY

To be successful, so far as is possible, and effective in discovering true values in the field of international affairs, Catholic international morality must express itself in two kinds of statements which must be distinguished before we go any further.

STATEMENTS OF ABSOLUTE TRUTH AND UNIVERSAL VALUES

First, the Catholic moralist is bound to give expression, in a "pure state", so to speak, to transcendent truths and values which are in no way contingent. For, although they are transcendent, they should nevertheless give a definite direction to all international politics throughout the varying historical circumstances.

Looked at from a Catholic point of view, these unvarying moral rules are divided into two classes:

1. Some aim to translate into action truths and values of the *natural order*. These are, at least theoretically, dis-

coverable by reason; but they can be clearly perceived only with the help of the Church.

2. The second kind aim to express *supernatural* truths and values known by the revelation of Christ. To these international affairs, and the whole life of man, should necessarily yet freely conform. They derive their unyielding firmness from the unchanging truth of the Mystery, to which the Catholic moralist bears witness for politicians.

These universal and unchanging statements, both in the natural and the supernatural order, present certain characteristics which must now be set out.

1. They have a fundamental place in Catholic international morality, since they should always and everywhere inspire the behaviour of States and of statesmen.

2. They are usually very general statements.

3. There are relatively few of them.

4. For the Catholic moralist they demand from politicians complete assent, since they only express the sure demands of human nature and the Mystery of Salvation, to which international affairs must be subordinated.

THE MORALIST'S "HISTORICO-PRUDENTIAL" SUGGESTIONS

About this nucleus of unvarying and universal principles, which are the doctrinal core of Catholic international morality, there is a group of assertions we can call, for want of a better name, "historico-prudential". Such assertions, or suggestions, which are the product of a kind of moral wisdom or prudence, do not aim directly and specifically to define and express in a pure state absolute and transcendent truths and values. Their proper aim is to ensure through that moral wisdom and prudence the effective sociological application of categorical truths and values in the changing and unforeseeable circumstances of ever-evolving historical events.

All books on international morality—those of Vitoria, Suarez and Taparelli, for example—are full of statements of this kind. It is therefore important, to avoid confusing them with absolute principles, to emphasize certain of their specific characteristics.

1. They can take two forms. They can assume that of *moral judgements of concrete historical realities* (facts, structures, doctrines) in the light of the unchanging truths and values given by the first category of assertions. Or they may take the form of *concrete rules of conduct* formulated by the political moralist, in order that politics shall enshrine unchanging values in all the changing events of history.

2. Logically regarded, such "historico-prudential" assertions have a hybrid character. They include in their very structure, and indissolubly, a simultaneous double reference: to the absolute and unvarying values which ought to be given material form in history; and to the contingent and changing historical circumstances in which these values must take that material form. So that looked at in one way, they seem to be absolute, categorical and unchanging assertions, because of the values they bear witness to; and looked at in another way they seem to be characterized by the historical contingency of the circumstances they refer to.

They show this hybrid character when they take the form of moral judgements of concrete circumstances. For example, the "historico-prudential" judgement of the function of the United Nations Organization in 1961 looks like a categorical and unchangeable assertion, since it stresses the absolute value of an international organization which must be effectively directed for the common good of humanity. But it also looks like a contingent assertion, belonging to a particular time, since it refers to a situation which was contingent and belonged to a particular time: the structure and function of U.N.O. in 1961.

This logically hybrid quality also affects the moralist's

"historico-prudential" assertions when they take the form of rules of conduct. We may take as an example the rule that the "developed" nations should help the "under-developed". Considered from one point of view, this is an indisputable and unchangeable translation of the absolute value judgement that "it is wrong that the division of wealth among peoples should be systematically unequal". Yet at the same time, looked at from other point of view, it is contingent and dated, since the state of the division of wealth among the nations of the world in 1961, which it seeks to alter, is itself a contingent historical fact.

It is important to notice this logical hybridity of "historico-prudential" judgements and rules in international morality, since it is in the light of this that we can settle the confused arguments which arise over the scope of the assertions of Catholic international morality.

3. Their third characteristic lies in the fact that the reference to the contingent, localized and dated facts which is contained, along with the reference to categorical, universal and unchangeable values, in the "historico-prudential" judgements and rules of international morality, can be threefold. It can, firstly, be a reference to *phenomena*, which change with time (for example, modern war is not exactly the same as war in the past). Secondly, it can be a reference to *institutions*, which vary as do all historical facts (for example, international organization in the time of U.N.O. is not the same historical reality as it was in the time of the League of Nations). Lastly, it can be a reference to *ideologies*, which themselves change despite the unchanging labels they wear (for example, nationalism as it now shows itself in nations lately colonies but now becoming independent is not quite the same as the nationalism of the colonizing nations in the nineteenth century, the age of colonization).

4. The same urgency and importance is not given by the moralist to all the "historico-prudential" judgements or

rules he propounds. His judgements, all within international morality, may have all degrees of logical strictness, from the assertion of a certainty to the statement of a simple probability; his rules sometimes have the force of definitive imperatives, sometimes that of emphatic advice, and sometimes only that of suggestions.

5. Because of these four characteristics, the "historico-prudential" judgements and rules of international morality may often, as opposed to the assertions of absolute principles, have an air of indecision or uncertainty. Within the orthodoxy of unchanging values they appeal to, some may leave room for a number of concrete choices, all allowable, in the context of the often unforeseeable historical circumstances they deal with. The concrete judgements or rules suggested by the Catholic moralist are not necessarily, therefore, the only valid ones, nor even always the most adequate. Such "historico-prudential" judgements and rules will have less of an absolute character the more they depend on the technical analysis of the facts of a given international situation, for the Catholic moralist has, if one may express it so, no particular "grace of infallibility" in such technical analysis.

It can be seen from all that we have said that Catholic international morality cannot be a homogeneous and rigid theory, leaving politicians no room to differ. If its value-judgements cannot be twisted round at will, as bias or prejudice can give a particular slant to ambiguous instructions, it nevertheless resembles a sort of spectrum of potential judgements of various shades varying from strong imperatives to suggestions that are open to discussion and revision.

THE CATHOLIC MORALIST'S SOURCES

To formulate his teachings, his imperatives, his judgements, his advice and his suggestions, the Catholic moralist must, obviously, take his inspiration from the writings of recent popes on international affairs. In our time, especially since Benedict XV, the papacy has been itself very concerned to formulate that teaching, those imperatives, judgements, advice and suggestions. Every Catholic moralist should therefore be as faithful a reflector as possible of contemporary popes' teachings on the community of nations. In the pages that follow, we shall try not to fall short in this duty.

One thing needs to be said if this book is not to mislead the reader. Our prime concern in it will be to stress the absolute principles involved in international morality.

On the other hand, we shall be brief concerning the prudential judgements and wise rules which the moralist is led to formulate by the contemporary international situation. This is because such "historico-prudential" assertions would necessitate, if they were to be fully relevant, analyses of such a length that there would be no room for them in so small a book.

CHAPTER IV

THE BASES OF CATHOLIC INTERNATIONAL MORALITY

Contemporary Catholic international morality rests in the first place on certain fundamental facts of doctrine and the general political laws which follow directly from them, and, secondly, on certain fundamental historical judgements which, in the light of that doctrine, the moralist brings to bear on the present world situation. These two sets of ideas will be considered in this chapter.

FUNDAMENTAL DOCTRINES AND THE GENERAL POLITICAL LAWS WHICH FOLLOW FROM THEM

All the particular laws of Catholic international morality today depend on one supreme necessity, the need for unity and communion which the whole of mankind must satisfy if it is to fulfil its true vocation. Before he does anything else the Catholic moralist must make certain doctrinal assertions on this subject.

First doctrinal assertion: In virtue of a natural vocation, that is, a necessity built into the very nature of man by the Creator, mankind must tend towards forming of itself one true family.

In his first encyclical, *Summi Pontificatus*, Pius XII,

continuing in the tradition of Benedict XV and Pius XI, strongly emphasized the natural necessity incumbent on all men and nations to think of themselves as, and to desire to be, united in the same way as are the members of the body or the children of one family. This, he implies, is a duty deeply rooted in the design of God the Creator of mankind, a duty deriving from the sovereign and absolute will of God, its character of categorical and universal urgency. He returned to the same theme in his Christmas message of 1944: "All peoples are destined to form one great human family, directed to the perfection of all, through helping one another, through sharing equitably the treasure of good things God has entrusted to man."

Moreover, to perceive where the basis of this duty lies there is absolutely no need, at least in law, to appeal to faith, properly so called. Reason is sufficient, which only needs to interpret, rightly and faithfully, the signs written by God into the nature of man. All men, endowed with freedom and with reason, are made by the same God in his own image, and by this kinship of origin and essence are plainly destined to share in the same end. Humanity cannot, therefore, realize its full potentialities, become what it should be according to its essential nature, except on the condition that the different peoples which make up mankind be bound together in an interdependence which does not involve relationships of conflict or opposition but expresses and gives practical form to the fundamental unity of mankind.

The Pope of Peace returned again and again to this natural moral law and its urgency.[1] In doing so, he was

---

[1] It should be noticed that in Pius XII's writings, as in those of the great Scholastics, "human nature" does not refer only to a set of observable phenomena to be collected and noted, but also to a *complex of values* which has to be taken into account. So the word "nature" does not mean what it does in contemporary science's references to "laws of nature".

only continuing a long tradition going back to St Augustine[2] through St Thomas,[3] Vitoria,[4] Suarez[5] and the modern Catholic doctors of "natural law" such as Taparelli d'Azeglio.[6] In the necessity for mankind to form one brotherly family, all these teachers see first and foremost a *natural law*.

Second doctrinal assertion: This natural and rational law is infinitely deepened and strengthened by the light shed on the supernatural vocation of mankind by the Revelation in Christ.

Since that revelation, mankind is called to make itself the Mystical Body of Christ. Of course, this supernatural vocation is a freely-given grace of God. It may be admitted, hypothetically, that God could have made a mankind whose free and reasonable members, while having to subordinate their actions to God's will, would not have been enabled by him to live their proper, full life through the mediation of Christ.[7] But in fact, man as he is, despite sin, which stains his history, and because of the redemption, which delivers him from sin, is actually and entirely able and bound to live the very life of the living God, who is Love. A history of man, therefore, which was not the story of mankind ordained in the thought and plan of God to the communion of all men under the breath of the Spirit of Love, would be a purely imaginary history.

It is true that the organization adequate for this supernatural communion, in the love and the life of the Godhead, of all men, who are all ordained—even if it be by the

2 *De Civ. Dei*, XIX. 7,12, etc.
3 *Summa Theol.*, II^a II^{ae} , q. 57, a. 3, and q. 95.
4 Vitoria, *De potestate civili;* Lyons, 1557.
5 Suarez, *De legibus* II.
6 See his *Saggio teoretico di diritto naturale*, 2nd edn, 1883, Bk. VI, art. 1, chapters i–iv, on the bases of the duty of mutual goodwill which nations should show to each other in times of peace and even in times of war.
7 Encyclical of Pius XII, *Humani Generis*, sections 1–4 (trans. Mgr R. A. Knox, C.T.S., 1950).

unconscious desire of their nature[8]—to become living members of the Body of Christ, is not a natural and secular institution like other political and economic institutions, juridically supra- or inter-national: it is simply the Church.

Nevertheless, the law of supernatural love and divine charity, which governs all men without exception as a matter of compelling grace—all men, these children of God at present scattered[9]—must be expressed and given shape on every level of secular life itself. It should animate the whole of temporal life with its spirit. Thus, so far as men refuse to make one world-wide family, they not only cheat their own *nature* of fulfilment but also reject their *supernatural* vocation, freely granted to them and enjoined on them by God; they are not only wrong about the values natural to their being, discoverable by reason, but also the supernatural values of their destiny, revealed by Christ and written by God into the heart of existence and of history.

So Pius XII, in his Christmas messages, taught that if men should form into one, true community, this was not only because of a natural law of solidarity, but also because of the divine law of charity, revealed by Christ and his Gospel; and the same point has been made by many contemporary Catholic moralists.

Third doctrinal assertion: From the first two assertions there follows a third: racialism is inadmissible.

Although modern anthropologists find it difficult to distinguish the idea of Race in any accurately scientific or objective way, mankind does obviously seem to be made up of several "races"—white, yellow, black; or Aryan, non-Aryan, Jewish, etc.

Now racialism is a mental outlook tending to deny the fundamental equality of all these "races", with respect to

[8] Cf. St Paul, Rom. 2. 14–16; Pius XII, encyclical *Mystici Corporis Christi* (C.T.S., 1950).
[9] John, 11. 52.

their nature, their value and their vocation. It holds that certain "races" have not been called, in the same way as others, to make up the human family. In every field of life and action it seeks to refuse to these "races" that it considers "inferior" their own proper place in the concert of mankind.

The Catholic moralist, as much in the name of his philosophy of nature as in that of the supernatural doctrine of the Mystical Body of Christ as it is expressed in the New Testament, and particularly in St Paul,[10] must adamantly refuse to accept such discrimination as unjustifiable either by reason or by faith. We remember how strongly, in the face of Hitler's racialism, Pius XI condemned this ideology in his encyclical *Mit Brennender Sorge* as the negation of the idea of mankind and the rejection of the calling of all men to unity. "The revelation of Christ cannot be ousted or supplanted by arbitrary revelations such as certain propagandists today claim to derive from what they call the Myth of Racial Purity."

Fourth doctrinal assertion: The "family" which the nations of the earth have to make a reality must not, however, be identified with a uniformity which would destroy the original genius of the various nations within it.

Such a uniformity, such a social levelling, supposing it to be possible at all, would involve, according to the view of the Church, the popes, and Catholic moralists, a double betrayal.

1. *A betrayal of the fundamental laws of human nature.* It is true that men are joined together in the same essential conditions of reason and freedom, and that mankind is bound to show in its collective behaviour that it recognizes its own natural unity; but if mankind wishes to become in

10 "No more Jew or Gentile, no more slave or freedman, no more male or female; you are all one person in Jesus Christ" (Gal. 3. 28; cf. Coloss. 3. 11).

history what it ought naturally to become, then within that unity it must develop and maintain a pluralism of complementary cultures. This natural and necessary cultural pluralism is very obvious at the individual level: for each man, though all are bound to behave as far as they can in the same way as free and reasonable creatures, is also bound by the uniqueness of his own temperament and personality to become "the most irreplaceable of creatures". The same obligation also rests on nations: their concert, if one may express it so, should be a polyphony which demands for its harmony a diversity of tones and parts.

2. *A betrayal of the fundamental demands of the supernatural.* The Mystical Body of Christ, which mankind is able to become because of the freely given but compelling grace of God, implies the communion of all the members of Christ in charity. But this gathering in the same Spirit, the same Light, the same Love, demands the preservation of complementary yet different personalities within the same divine life. In his Epistles (Rom. 12; 1 Cor. 12) St Paul makes this supernatural demand quite clear. So true is this that the Church militant here on earth, which is already in germ and in promise the Church triumphant in heaven, while striving to gather all the nations of the world into the unity of the same faith, the same love, the one fold, through the same baptism and the same Bread (1 Cor. 10. 17; 12. 13; Ephes. 14. 4 6), strives also not only not to eliminate but even to preserve and give greater life to the original civilizations encountered in her expansion.[11] During the second World Congress of African writers and artists in Rome in April, 1959, Pope John XXIII said the same:

> The Church is not to be identified with any culture, not even that western culture with which her history is so closely bound

[11] In *The Catholic Spirit*, in this series, André Rétif, S.J., makes very clear the claim of the Church to save not only every man but all that is human.

up. For her mission is of another order: that of the religious
salvation of man. But the Church, full of a youth ever renewed
by the breath of the Spirit, is always ready to recognize and
welcome and even give life to all that belongs to the honour of
the intelligence and heart of man on all the shores of the world,
besides those of the Mediterranean basin, which was, under
Providence, the cradle of Christianity.

So Catholicism claims that the religious and supernatural salvation of mankind demands that a certain
sociological diversity be preserved among the nations of the
world even at the natural level. Mankind must be a family
containing its own diversity, not only because it is called to
be a true "human family", but because it is also called to
be a true "divine family". In both cases the very idea of a
family implies that there should be preserved, under the
father's aegis, the diversity of the children.

So Pius XII was right to stress in his encyclical *Summi
Pontificatus* that it is required, both by respect for natural
values and by respect for supernatural values, that the ideal
of the unity of mankind—the prime importance of which
ideal demands the effort of all men everywhere—must not
be confused with the chimera of a uniformity which is
superficial and external and thereby debilitating.[12]

From this very general teaching on the community of
mankind and the supreme ideal of unity, there follow
certain fundamental laws for contemporary States, which
can be summarized in this way.

*First law: While States should preserve the right to a
genuine sovereignty, they must move towards the formation of
a true inter-State community of them all, provided each is
willing to accept the limitations on its own sovereignty which
become necessary in the international field.*

[12] The same point is made by John XXIII in his encyclical *Mater
et Magistra*, Part III, Section 2.

The law of unity and universal charity, which we have just described and which governs all mankind, has certain essential applications in the field of the *relations between individuals*. An individual who is fully aware of that law can no longer ever think of "foreigners" except as "brothers". But the same law of love applies to *States*, and requires that their relations should be those of understanding, of agreement and mutual help. On the morrow of the First World War, Benedict XV reminded the governments of the time that the Gospel precept of charity has a value for States comparable to that which it has for individuals.[13]

It would be fanciful to imagine that individuals could attain to that ideal of communion among themselves which both the natural law and the law of Christ demand that they pursue here on earth, if *States*, within which the individual lives his life, ignored one another or even developed relations of systematic hostility. The effects of war—hot or cold—which our generations have suffered and are suffering, show plainly that individual charity can work only with difficulty or incompletely in an international situation in which States do not enter into or do not remain in a condition of real inter-State community.

This duty of States to form a community must not be understood in too simple a sense. Since the unity of mankind must not become a "debilitating uniformity", to use Pius XII's words, an international community must allow to exist within it a real political diversity. What does this mean? Not only that it must not end by suppressing the diversity of its member-States, but that it should normally require the existence of all kinds of intermediate communities, of very varying forms. Contemporary examples are the British Commonwealth, the European Economic

13 Encyclical *Pacem*, 1920.

Community, and other existing federations or confederations. Too strict and narrow an idea of the unity of a world community would endanger the legitimate links between States which have cultural, geographic or economic affinities, more or less close, with others.

The ideal international community should therefore exist in a state of tension between two poles: the preservation within mankind of a number of different States or groups of States, and the establishment of organic links binding these into a world-wide whole ordered for the good of all nations.

Second law: The highest political value, which should rule the conduct of States in their mutual relations, should therefore be the good of the community of States, the universal common good of humanity.

In other words, each and every government should so order its international relations as to assist in bringing into being, maintaining and developing conditions favourable to the establishment of this community of States.

True, the policies of any government should be *immediately* inspired by the particular common good of its own people, as Leo XIII said in his encyclical *Immortale Dei*. And it is also true that in order to fulfil that function, which is its immediate *raison d'être*, each State must possess, and permanently possess, true internal autonomy. International law is thus responsible, in the field of this internal life of each State, for seeing that each is "independent" with regard to the particular authority of any other State. It is in this sense that we can and should hold to the phrase so often used in recent years: peoples—and States, which are the judicial expression of these population groups—have the right to conduct their own affairs themselves.

But that being said, the particular common good of each State cannot be rightly understood or correctly evaluated by its rulers unless it is considered in its necessary context, that of the common good of all the nations of the world.

In short, the Catholic moralist denies any valid opposition between the good of the international community and the good of each nation. In fact, the two come up against one another and affect one another in much the same way as do the good of the individual and that of the various natural communities (family, professional, communal and so on) in which he lives and in which he finds the social conditions of his own development. A man cannot preserve his own personality if within the family, for example, he indulges all the whims of his own fancy; on the other hand, the family is itself destroyed if its common life stamps out the originality of each of its members. In the same way, a world super-State which utterly abolished intermediate authorities would betray the particular common good of each people as well as the general common good; whereas if the sovereignty of particular States were unconditional and unrestricted the establishment of a true international community would be impossible, a community, that is, in which each people could find the most general conditions of its own development. All this was said nearly forty years ago by Louis Le Fur:

> As has been rightly said, the common good is both immanent in the individual and transcendent. This amounts to saying that, as opposed to a too common opinion, there is no opposition between the good and sound aims of individuals and those of the State. If there is sometimes, or even often, an apparent opposition, that is because of excessive or ill-based claims of one or the other. For example, the individual may refuse to share the equitably distributed national responsibilities, or even, in time of war, may claim that the interests of his country, which are also his own, should be defended by others while he himself stands to profit by their success without running any personal risk. Similar excessive or ill-based claims are met

with on the part of the State, both with respect to its own nationals, by the abuse of its powers, and in respect of other States, as in the case of a State which wants to enjoy the advantages of international society without accepting the responsibilities which are their necessary counterpart. But to look at it this way is wrong: it is too narrow and selfish. Man is a social individual, and can only develop in society; the potentialities, and the field of action of civilized man are vastly greater in his civilized society than those of the "savage". Exactly the same should be true of the State within the society of nations. As in any well-ordered society, the power and the security of its elements, far from being diminished, will be greatly increased. In normal conditions this is precisely the final aim and the first result of every well-constructed and well-directed association. At the level of independence achieved now by modern States, life in society is almost as necessary to them as it is to individuals.[14]

Third law: This universal common good includes a whole hierarchy of values, fixed by the nature and vocation of man.

The universal common good is a complex value. It includes a series of demands ranged in order which impose themselves on mankind because of what man is by nature and of what he ought to become by his calling.

At the bottom of this ladder of values are demands in the *economic* order. Material wealth should be shared among the different nations, large and small, in an equitable way. The position with regard to the possession of the resources of the world (producer and consumer goods, raw materials, etc.) by different nations is very much the same as that within each State with regard to private property belonging to individuals. If each State is normally bound to assure for its own nationals the administration of the wealth of its own territory, nevertheless the goods of the earth are meant for

---

[14] "Le problème du Nationalisme et de l'Internationalisme au regard de la Morale, et du Droit Naturel," in *Semaine Sociale du Havre*, 1926, p. 302.

all and must be used with regard to the general well-being of the whole human race.[15]

But those materialist views, today only too widespread, according to which these economic demands are the only values of the common good we have to promote, are very far from the truth. An ideal international order must also consider the *cultural* development of all peoples in all nations. For man is not only body: he is also mind and intellect. So, in this field, nations must help one another so that mankind as a whole may progress to ever higher levels of civilization, while preserving the original character and genius of each people.

These values of material prosperity and cultural advancement, however, are themselves bound up with values properly belonging to the *spiritual* order. An international order must be one of loyalty and justice and of mutual respect among the nations; it must be an order of fidelity, *rebus sic stantibus*, to contracts, and an order of liberty; and it must be an order of security and of peace. Taken by itself, a state of international affairs in which nations attack one another and compete commercially and fight among themselves, is an inhuman state, one betraying both the ideal of solidarity desired by the nature of man and the ideal of divine charity demanded by the Church. It is such as to endanger the sowing on earth of the seeds of the eternal community of the Kingdom of God which, in the general view of Christians, must "germinate" here below.

The international common good could thus be defined as the sum of those inter-State relations (economic, political, cultural and spiritual) which enable mankind to become what it ought to become in the light of all that it is by nature and by vocation.

[15] Pius XII, Christmas message, 1941; Pius XII, referring to the common enjoyment of the wealth of the world, took up again ideas that Vitoria had long ago expounded in the theory of the *ius communicationis* in his *De Indis*.

"HISTORICO-PRUDENTIAL" JUDGEMENTS OF THE PRESENT WORLD SITUATION

During recent years the peoples of the world have become more and more aware of these basic doctrinal positions concerning the unity of human nature and of the fundamental political laws which subordinate the behaviour of individual nations to the pursuit of the common good of all the world. This has happened because of certain facts of the situation which are easily discerned and described.

The birth of the idea of the "universal coexistence" of nations

Thanks to the discovery and perfection of modern techniques of communication and information (press, radio, television, faster transport, etc.) and thanks to the various cooperative efforts different nations of the world have made together to increase man's scientific control of the material world, the last twenty years or so have seen the awakening of a deep awareness of the oneness of the many nations, their *coexistence*. What does this mean? Only recently, what happened in Europe seemed to an African or an Asian or a South American to belong to a different world from his own; and similarly, for a European what happened in Asia or Africa or South America seemed to be happening in a different world. We could perhaps go further: thirty or forty years ago, the African, Asian or South American *did not know* what was happening in Europe; Europe did not really exist for them. And the European did not know what was going on in Africa, Asia or South America: his horizons, the field of his human cares and worries, did not go beyond the borders of his own continent. So each people tended to regard itself as a single, closed little world, looking on its own country as a world shut in, like a microcosm without any context.

Things are different now. Whatever the people we belong to, all know and feel that that people is one in a context, in the midst of a multitude of other peoples all as real and living as our own; and the context now extends to include all the world.

The birth of the idea of the "mutual interdependence" of nations

This feeling of our real coexistence carries with it the feeling of our real interdependence. Besides the technical causes we have already mentioned, it is perhaps two world wars and other such disasters which have brought forth this sense of the real solidarity of all men. We have learnt from them and now know that a conflict beginning anywhere in the world can and might have repercussions at the ends of the earth and affect the lives of every nation. Again, the development of economic exchanges and the extension of international markets have emphasized this awareness of the universal interdependence of the peoples of mankind. Such an enormous crisis as the American depression of 1929, which affected the whole world, has shown us that the economic situation of any nation is affected by that of every other. So every clear-sighted observer of our times can see that the life of any nation is conditioned by factors covering the whole world, belonging to mankind as a whole. So the idea of absolute independence, using the term in a strict sense, whether of individuals or nations, is seen to be false, from many points of view, false and out of keeping with the facts. In reality, the fate of any man and any nation depends, willy-nilly, on the fates of others, of all the others.

The birth of the hope for an ideal of unity and agreement among the nations

The ever-sharper appreciation of the first two factual judgements—the actual coexistence and interdependence of the nations of the world—has caused hope to spring in men's hearts: hope that it may be possible to create among all the nations of the world, necessarily coexistent and necessarily interdependent as they are, a true brotherly unity. The facts that the nations do coexist and are inter-dependent—facts we can see only too plainly even through the "cold war" which poisons the contemporary inter-national atmosphere—can be and are true even among situations of strife and conflict. What coexistence there actually is, is not necessarily and of itself peaceful or peace-making; nor is the actual interdependence of the nations necessarily or automatically a brotherly interdependence. But if we look at the broad sweep of world opinion, man-kind today wants the nations of the world to coexist in peace, and wants the ties of interdependence to be ties of peace, of brotherly feeling and cooperation.

As proof of the existence of this ideal and hope, we can point to the many efforts which have been made during the last few years, of which we shall soon have more to say, to substitute, for the anarchical relationships of competition and opposition between nations, relationships organized on the basis of mutual understanding and agreement and of concerted collaboration on common tasks.

Now for the Catholic moralist and the Church to whose authority he appeals, this hope and ideal are only the conscious awareness—more or less confused but also more or less immediate, and fundamentally very relevant at this time—of a *value*, of a true *vocation* of man, which Christian philosophy and Catholic theology have for so long been concerned to make clear and emphasize.

What is more, this conscious awareness, in the eyes of the Catholic moralist and of the Church, makes possible the setting-up today of international institutions which would perhaps have been impossible yesterday when things were not so clear. The relevance and the importance of inter-national morality are therefore easily seen today; not only because of the transcendent doctrinal truths it must contain, or because of the categorical imperatives it puts forward, but also because of the new possibilities offered by contemporary history for research into, and for some success of, an effective international morality.

CHAPTER V

THE INTERNATIONAL COMMUNITY AND INTERNATIONAL ORGANIZATION

Granted the general ideas that underlie Catholic international morality, which we have just been describing, the Catholic moralist is bound to take up a definite attitude to the question of a world organization. But it must be admitted that this extraordinarily complex question is still, in many respects, subject to some uncertainties of mind, so that the views of contemporary Catholic moralists on it form a sort of spectrum, ranging from a few categorical assertions to certain "historico-prudential" judgements on the international organizations actually created in history and capable of being examined, and passing through some philosophical considerations of a directive kind which the moralist is the first to recognize as subject to critical discussion, and as capable of innumerable concrete realizations difficult to be precise about *a priori*.

The categorical assertions demand absolute agreement, in his eyes, since they are only the expressions, as adequate as possible, of absolute, universal and transcendent values.

The directive, philosophical considerations he believes merit some attention, for although they cannot claim to be infallibly right, they are attempts to express what seems to the reason to be a collection of the probably permanent demands of human nature.

As for the judgements relating to existing international organizations, to their working, their actual, contemporary administration, to the historical possibility of improving them in this or that way, and so on, such judgements also, we must recognize, are necessarily temporary and open to discussion and revision. The moralist must admit that these judgements must be submitted to constant adjustment, since the very institutional realities they relate to and seek to improve are changing and developing, ceaselessly altering their shape under the unforeseeable pressures of history. They are something like clouds in the sky changing their shape under the influence of the wind, which blows this way and that, while we cannot always know exactly where it is blowing from or, especially, where to.

The present chapter will thus fall into three distinct parts: in the first, we shall set out the doctrinal principles, few and general as they are, which the contemporary moralist, at any rate, regards as binding on States and the men who represent them, now and in any future historical situation. In the second, we shall set out some of the considerations of a directive kind which the moralist can draw by reflection from the philosophical study of the nature of man and the demands that nature seems to make on the level of international political morality. And in the third part, we shall set out some "historico-prudential" judgements on the United Nations Organization and its specialized institutions. These judgements, let us repeat, will present that hybrid character we have already stressed. Since they refer, so far as is possible, to transcendent values in assessing historical facts, they will seem from one point of view to be imperatives, because of those values. But from the other side they will look like assertions of the same historical contingency as the institutions they deal with; and as such they will be subject to constant revision and should be formulated only with due modesty.

So we shall try to set out and distinguish in this chapter these three parts of present-day Catholic morality dealing with international organization. For our inspiration, particularly in the first part, we shall draw on the statements of contemporary popes.

DOCTRINAL PRINCIPLES

First principle: Mankind is today bound to try to establish and run as good an international organization as possible, now that the state of world affairs makes it possible.

The last clause is easily explained. Moralists and others, particularly politicians, are faced and can only be faced with the problem of international organization in a progressive manner. The problem cannot come before the mind before the gradual fulfilment of the historical conditions making it possible for States to cooperate effectively within an organized society; that is to say, before the sufficient development of world communications.

Besides this, the question of a world organization of nations could not take shape before the appearance of the modern nation-State. The first theologian who had any insight into the moral problems which such an organization would pose was the Spanish Dominican Francisco de Vitoria (*c.* 1485–1546), universally recognized as the father of international law in his two works *De Indis* and *De jure belli*. After Vitoria and his Jesuit compatriot Francisco Suarez (1548–1617), we have to wait until the nineteenth century for another theologian to take up again the moral problem of international organization: the Italian Jesuit Taparelli d'Azeglio (1793–1862).

Contemporary historical circumstances have led the

popes—those moralists in St Peter's chair—to work out with unprecedented breadth and fullness the principles which should govern the international organization now being built up. Now the first principle, which they have affirmed ever more strongly, is that the international organization of nations is today as "natural" and as "necessary" as the nation-State itself. The Code of Political Morality of Malines, which sums up admirably the thought of recent sovereign pontiffs, says that it "corresponds to the progressive natural tendencies of man and of nations. No State today has the right to opt out, for it is not for the will to contradict the laws of nature or oppose progress."

Pius XII was eloquent and clear on this subject. Looking at the historical facts of our times he, who was so justly called the Pope of Peace, stressed whenever he could the urgent need for a world organization. These pontifical pronouncements should be borne in mind by Catholic moralists, for they do but give expression to a natural necessity, the conditions for the satisfaction of which are all now present together. It is this natural necessity which throws into strong relief the tragedies and threats of our time.

When war began in 1939, four years before any attempt to organize another international body to replace the decayed League of Nations, Pius XII said that to establish true peace again, once the armed conflict then beginning was over, "there would have to be a stable and fruitful organization such as men of good will have always longed for, an organization which, because it respected the laws of God, could ensure that all nations, large and small, were mutually independent, could insist on faithful adherence to genuine agreements, and could preserve, among the efforts of each for the prosperity of all, the healthy freedom and dignity of the human person".[1]

[1] Reply of November 10th, 1939, to the new ambassador of the Republic of Haiti.

In his first Christmas message in 1939 he reviewed the fundamental points of a just and lasting peace and returned to this theme of the creation or rebuilding of international institutions. In a broadcast of September 1st, 1944, when the end of the Second World War was in sight, and when the Allies gathered at Dumbarton Oaks were working out the first ideas of the United Nations, the same pope told the world of his satisfaction in seeing such a project taking shape; and in his Christmas message of that year, when he had seen the resolutions taken by the international commissions assembled to draw up the first draft of the Charter of San Francisco, he wished this preparatory work all success.

When the Charter was signed and came into force in October, 1945, Pius XII prayed that, though it had been born of the solidarity of the war, it would enlarge its scope. At Christmas, 1948, he wrote: "May the United Nations Organization become the full and pure expression of peaceful international solidarity, wiping out of its statutes and its institutions all trace of its origins, which necessarily lay in the solidarity of wartime."

In fact, the working of the United Nations Organization in the years that followed showed up the defects of its institution. But although he expressed his sorrow at these defective aspects, he never allowed the existence of such an international organization to be called in question. Shortly before his death, he wrote in his Christmas message of 1956:

If we refer to certain defects in the working of the United Nations Organization it is because we should like to see the authority of that organization strengthened, especially in order to achieve general disarmament. It is only within the framework of an organization such as U.N.O. that the undertaking of each nation to reduce its armaments and especially to give up the production and use of certain kinds of weapons could be given in common concord and made into a strict obligation in international law. In the same way, only the United Nations is at present in a position to demand the observance of such an agreement, by assuring the effective control of the armaments of each and every nation without exception.

We may note in passing that Pius XII in all this was following the example of his predecessors Leo XIII and Benedict XV, for it has been a constant mark of the history of the papacy that the sovereign pontiffs have desired and encouraged and supported all efforts made towards the establishment of an international organization since the beginning of the nineteenth century. Pius XI, while he saw quite clearly that the League of Nations fell short of what was needed so long as the nations of the world gave insufficient public recognition to the sacred character of law, nevertheless concerned himself greatly with the working of that body, approving its principle and recognizing its necessity.

Catholic international morality, therefore, if it is to move in agreement with the thought of these popes, cannot allow this basic affirmation to be weakened: the effective ordering of the polity of each nation towards the common, international good demands today that there be an effective international organization of nations. For the Catholic moralist this position is now irrefutably established.

Second principle: This moral necessity for an international organization of nations today is analogous to the moral necessity for the nation-State itself.

In fact, the effective pursuit of the international common good depends on conditions analogous to those on which depends the effective pursuit of the national common good. In the same way as the "desire to live in common for common ends", which characterizes a nation, tends spontaneously, and legitimately, except for effects which seriously harm other nations or the rest of the world, to avail itself of the whole complex juridico-political apparatus of the State, organized in order to express itself and develop, so the desire for an international community, which should animate the nations as a group, can only find a guaranteed stability through world political institutions which possess competent authority and which by their concerted action can assure the victory of the good of mankind over the particular interests of their member-States.

PHILOSOPHICAL CONSIDERATIONS

The methods and procedure of an international organization cannot be identical with that of a national organization, for although the two societies—that of the nation and the international society of nations—are analogous in structure, they are not identical. An international organization cannot work in exactly the same way as a nation-State, since it is not composed of exactly the same elements.

All the same, because of the analogy which does exist between the necessity, meaning and importance of national organization for the good of the nation's citizens, and the necessity, meaning and importance of a world international organization for the good of the nations of the world, the Catholic moralist can, to a certain extent, *mutatis mutandis*, construct a political philosophy of a world international organization by transposing, as it were, the ideas of the political philosophy of the State. We shall now sketch out a number of philosophical considerations of this kind, without making any sort of claim to be dogmatic, to have irrefutable evidence, or to have presented a complete picture of such a political philosophy.

1. It seems that the ideal—abstract enough, to be sure— towards which we should move as it were towards a limit, is the progressive establishment in history of a political World Government having real jurisdiction over individual

States. Without such an *institutional instrument* having legislative, executive, judiciary and penal powers so as to declare the rules (without ever reaching a state of completion) of international law, to see that they are carried out, to encourage those that obey them and to penalize those who break them, without this it is difficult to see how individual nations' politics could be fully coordinated. In short, there is the same pressing need for this World Government, other things being equal, as there is for government within the State in order to see, within the field of its proper powers, that the more restricted activities within the nation are harmonized.

2. But it would be wrong to think of this World Government as a "dictatorial" authority. That is, it would be quite wrong to envisage a World super-State, the powers of which were so unrestricted, so boundless, that it would amount to the total destruction of intermediate national authorities. With such a system, the legitimate and necessary diversity which should exist within mankind on the political as well as on the racial, cultural and spiritual levels, would be threatened with extinction in the name of the chimera of absolute political unity. We have already referred to Louis Le Fur's warning, given in 1926, against such oversimplified views, and the warning is still as much needed today: "The conception has been put forward of a super-State substituting its own sovereignty for that of individual nations; but such a solution should be rejected without hesitation".[2] If the totalitarian sovereignty of certain States is rightly criticized for swallowing up the intermediate bodies which make up the nation, surely we should not make such totalitarianism the rule, and set up another such sovereign authority, this time universal, and therefore much more dangerous still. The only acceptable solution is the

[2] Louis Le Fur, *art. cit.*, pp. 294 foll.

establishment of a World Government of such a type as to involve in its working the participation of the subordinate authorities of the member-States. This is perfectly possible provided, as is right, none of the admittedly real and proper State authorities is regarded as "perfectly" independent. A similar idea was put forward by Vitoria, of whose general principles Reuter writes: "only in the present day have they found formal expression in the League of Nations and the United Nations".[3]

3. All the same, such an eventual World Government ought to leave room, subordinated to itself but also with a certain autonomy, not only for nation-States but also for a whole body of specialized public organizations concerned with culture, health, the struggle against hunger, etc. The specifically political machinery of the central authority should see to their control, but not to their direct administration. In other words, the powers granted to the World Government should cover a certain field of action and should be confined within limits comparable to the limits and the field of action which Catholic political philosophy attributes to the political machinery of the State.[4]

We must be very careful [writes Robert Bosc, S.J.[5]] not to confuse the State in the general and philosophical sense, which can mean the whole body politic (that is, the people politically organized), with the State in the strict and narrow sense, used to mean the machinery of government (legislative, executive and penal). The first alone is the political society necessary to man. Jacques Maritain has shown what confusion of ideas was

3 Paul Reuter, *op. cit.*, p. 44.
4 On the field of action and the limits of the power of the political authority in the State, according to the traditional political philosophy of Catholicism, see Jacques Maritain, *Man and the State* (ed. by Richard O'Sullivan, Q.C., London, Hollis and Carter, 1954). On the analogy with the future World Government, see especially Chapter VII.
5 *La Société internationale et l'Église* (Spes, 1961), pp. 350–1.

produced in the sixteenth century by the substitution of the word "State" for *res publica* to designate the body politic. The State in the strict sense, in fact, is only a part of the body politic. "The State is only that part of the body politic especially concerned with the maintenance of law, the promotion of the common welfare and public order, and the administration of public affairs. The State is a part which *specializes* in the interests of the *whole* . . . The State is but an agency entitled to use power and coercion, and made up of experts or specialists in public order and welfare, an instrument in the service of men . . . When we say that the State is the superior part in the body politic, this means that it is superior to the other organs or collective parts in this body, but it does not mean that it is superior to the body politic itself. The part as such is inferior to the whole."[6] It is only by means of this distinction between the body politic and the State that we can escape the contradictions which, from the sixteenth century on, have beset liberal and totalitarian theories alike, and establish a truly political (not simply governmental) idea of the State, which will allow the people to control the State. Only through that distinction can we set up a fully *political* and not a purely *governmental* theory of the world community. In fact, if we were to forget that the fundamental political reality is the body politic and not the State, we should run the risk of ending, after a process of intergovernmental association, with an absolute Super-State or with a higher State with no body politic but simply superimposed on the life of the individual States that it controlled and fettered, even if it were created through elections and popular representation.

4. In order not to succumb to the temptation to become totalitarian, the eventual World Government should not only avoid swallowing up the national authorities subordinate to it and claiming to destroy all the autonomy of the specialized public organizations working in and around it, but should also take care not to prevent the birth and exercise of

[6] Maritain, *op. cit.*, pp. 10–11.

international authorities of a more particular kind (such as, for example, any future European authority), which communities created by history (geographic communities, economic, cultural, social and political communities and so on) may suggest be created or kept in being. Only by such pluralism can despotism in the World Government be avoided: for the most certain effect of such despotism would be to abolish, under the pretext of assuring international cohesion, the diversified richness of the true community of mankind.

5. Lastly, we can say that a World Government should leave plenty of room for private initiative. That is, it should allow to exist international organizations which are not governmental, provided it makes sure of a certain degree of coordination between these private organizations and the set of official, public institutions.

6. The establishment of such a World Government, so balanced, could not happen all at once; it might even take centuries. It may even be only a directive ideal, intended in the fullness of history to play the part of an "asymptote", to give a direction through the thread of events to the permanent effort of creation to which politicians ought to devote themselves. We must expect to see, in fact, only imperfect international organizations, imperfect as is all that is human, as are all existing national organizations. In other words, an international organization is a reality to be envisaged as one subject to continuous improvement. It would consequently be as well, surely, to provide in its institution the means and the procedure for its periodical revision.

7. Nevertheless, as Pius XII said, this rule must be laid down once for all: however imperfect it may be, an established World Government must possess the presumption of law in the decisions it takes which are within its proper competence. In every case, at any given point in history, what will settle the question of the value and legitimacy of

the then established international organization will be not so much what concrete form it has in fact assumed, but rather its ability, with that form, to take at that time effective care of the common good of the world, to the degree to which history then allows such care to be taken. It is only in cases of *manifest* abuse of power that States could legitimately dissent from the decisions it takes or from the recommendations it makes within the field of its powers. Only a clear betrayal of the common good of the whole by the established international authority could justify the disobedience of State authorities subordinated to it, since by committing such a betrayal the international authority would lose its very *raison d'être*. The demands of the common good of all nations are the only right foundation of its existence and of its powers. After all, such moral principles are only the logical transposition of those which Catholic political philosophy puts forward with regard to the obedience due to the government established in an individual State.

8. The immediate objects of a World Government are clearly determined, as are those of national political authorities, by the historical situation at any given time and the immediate demands of circumstances. In our time, these immediate objects are fairly clearly those which are set out in the Charter of the United Nations:

1. To achieve the end of colonial rule (Chapters XI, XII and XIII).
2. To prevent or resolve armed conflicts (IV, VII and VIII).
3. To establish the general conditions for cooperation among the nations, and so to abolish the present tragedy of underdevelopment (IX and X).

The second and third points will form the subjects of Chapters VII and VIII of this book.

9. The Catholic moralist must state one last important philosophical consideration. The establishment of international organizations as adequately constructed as possible and the determination of their immediate objects are *necessary* conditions for the effective pursuit of the common good of mankind, but they are not *sufficient* conditions. Besides these, and even prior to them, is the need for as unanimous a desire as possible, in the minds both of the governors of individual nations and of the officials of the existing international organizations, to realize a spiritual order of values.

To see that this is so, we recall what was said in Chapter II about the conditions under which a political decision can be regarded as a reasonable one: such a decision must rest on as accurate an assessment as possible of the facts of the situation—the starting point; secondly, it must also rest on as exact an account as possible of the technical means available (judicial, economic, political, diplomatic, military). But it is also necessary, and it is too often not recognized, that the governments involved agree on the transcendent values to be pursued.

So we repeat that the specific task of the Catholic moralist is not to undertake the factual and technical analysis of situations and methods—an analysis for which he has no special competence as a Catholic—but to remind politicians *urbi et orbi* of the values they must agree upon and the ethical rules which follow from those values and are universally binding on the consciences of men.

We shall therefore deal in Chapter VI with the genuinely political ethical rules, drawing largely on the writings of Pius XII.

CONTEMPORARY JUDGEMENTS

The Catholic moralist, in putting forward his conception of a morally desirable international organization, not only asserts certain principles and suggests certain ideas furnished by Christian political philosophy, but also tries to give a few contemporary judgements on the existing international organization, in the light of those principles and those ideas.

Assuming that the reader knows something about the United Nations Organization already,[7] we need only bring out the good and bad points, in a general way, of U.N.O. and its subordinate organizations, as they appear to us (in 1961) in the light of the principles and philosophical considerations we have just now set out.

U.N.O.'s good points

1. The first good point about U.N.O. is that it exists at all. It was this above all that Pius XII, in the texts we have referred to, was so eager to emphasize. So we can understand why it was that at a time when certain politicians were tempted to dismiss U.N.O. as of no importance, because of its administrative and structural difficulties and insufficiencies, the Cardinals and Archbishops of France declared, in October, 1960, that "whatever were the failings inherent in any human institution, however slow and laborious its workings, an international organization of nations is today more than ever indispensable to the establishment of peace in the world." It would thus be very wrong to make the failings of U.N.O. an excuse to undermine, more or less directly, its very existence. However imperfect, the United Nations Organization is very much better than nothing.

2. The authors of the United Nations Charter seem to have been conscious of the fact that the sovereignty of nations is not unconditional, and that, if not in the realm of a State's internal affairs at least in that of its foreign affairs,

[7] To obtain a general idea of the existing international organization, the reader must consult the Charter of the United Nations: see Select Bibliography, for this and other relevant works.

which concern the peace of the world, an international organization has every right, by the means described in Chapter VII of the Charter, to use its authority, *and if need be force*, against a State committing illegal actions. This represents an advance on the ideas behind the League of Nations, the member-States of which entirely preserved their absolute sovereignty.

3. But although they seem to have been careful in this way to ensure the real political autonomy of U.N.O., the authors of the Charter were also careful to avoid the possibility that that political authority might become "totalitarian" in any of the ways described above.

(*a*) Thus, the Charter states firmly that the sovereignty of the member-States may not be completely done away with (Chapter I, Art. 2, No. 7) and that the Security Council, before imposing by force on any nation conduct conforming to the law of nations, must try all means of negotiation, enquiry, mediation, arbitration, etc., to work out and adopt a reasonable international course of action.

(*b*) In the same sense, the text of the Charter foresees the establishment of specialized agencies (Art. 57) over which U.N.O. has no right of direct administration but only one of simple coordination (Art. 58).

(*c*) And again in the same sense, the Charter explicitly looks forward to the existence of regional organizations which shall eventually possess a certain political autonomy (Chapter VIII).

(*d*) In practice, the Charter leaves room for non-governmental organizations (such as the World Federation of Trades Unions, or the International Chamber of Commerce). In their case it is enough to ensure a certain degree of coordination between such "private" organizations and those of an official kind.

In short, the structure of U.N.O., in many ways, shows how conscious its authors were of the complex character of the "organized body politic of the world", the international machinery demanded by the nature of man.

It would be easy to give many more examples of the way in which the Charter of the United Nations has advanced beyond the position in the 1919 Covenant of the League of Nations.

The weaknesses of U.N.O.

All the same, U.N.O. has today (1961) a number of obvious weaknesses; Pius XII himself remarked on some of its failings in his Christmas message of 1956. Without claiming to be exhaustive or to sum up all that could be said, we shall set down and consider a few points of major importance.

1. The Security Council has lost all its authority and all possibility of manoeuvring, thanks to the abuse of the veto which is the right of the five permanent members.

2. Since the beginning of the Korean War the supreme executive has become, on the initiative of the U.S.A., the General Assembly in extraordinary session; U.N.O. thus has now all the weaknesses and divisions and the tardiness of rule by assembly.

3. There is a certain confusion of powers. For example, when U.N.O. has intervened between nations in conflict, such as between Israel and Egypt in 1956, has it undertaken a judicial or a political action, or both, or neither?

4. Are the complicated and purely theoretical procedures for control and sanctions envisaged in Chapter VII of the Charter, in order to ensure the correct execution of the decisions of the Security Council or the recommendations of the General Assembly, really effective?

In brief, is U.N.O., as it has, in fact, taken shape, really a World Government which can, in the name of the common good expressed in a code of international law properly established, effectively unify the policies of its member-States? Is it not rather a sort of world-wide diplomatic club, where the representatives of the member-States make speeches, often in a vacuum, or even, very often, get themselves hurt in the cut and thrust of debate?

Could not these failings, and many others, be due in the last resort not merely to the still very imperfect legal arrangements of a world institution, but much more to the fact that the member-States, and especially the opposed blocs of East and West, are by no means of one mind on the meaning of the fundamental spiritual values which should be politically aimed for?

The Catholic moralist is convinced this is the case. That is why, although he may, somewhat modestly, make such remarks about international organization as this chapter briefly suggests, he strives above all to make clear the spiritual foundation of international affairs, on which the member-States should base their actions for the good of the world. It is this indispensable spiritual basis which forms the subject of the next chapter.

CHAPTER VI

THE INTERNATIONAL COMMUNITY AND ITS SPIRITUAL BASIS

The effective and concerted pursuit of the universal common good demands the progressive establishment of a balanced World Government as well adapted as possible to the shifting circumstances of history; it must be made increasingly effective by the constant and patient labours of construction and administration of a world-wide institutional apparatus which respects the complexity of a truly human "organized body politic". The urgent need for such a World Government has, we hope, been sufficiently stressed in the last chapter.

But the establishment of such an institutional apparatus, although it is a necessary condition, is not a sufficient one. It is also necessary, on a level which is no longer institutional or legal, but spiritual, that there should be as unanimous agreement of minds as possible on the recognition of true spiritual values, and as fervent an agreement of wills as possible in the pursuit of those values.

In his Christmas message of 1942, Pius XII proclaimed this need for spiritual unanimity:

Never has it been so capitally important to understand clearly the true foundations of all social life as in these days when humanity, diseased by the poison of social errors and perversions and tossed by a fever of conflicting desires, doctrines, and aims, has become the unhappy prey of a disorder created by itself, and is experiencing the disruptive effects of false social theories that neglect and contravene the laws of God. Just as darkness with all its oppressive horrors cannot be dispelled by a will-o'-the-wisp but only by the light, so disorder can be banished only by order, and by an order that is not fictitious but real. Only in one way can we hope for salvation, renewal, and true progress, and that is through the return of numerous and influential sections of mankind to a true conception of society, a return which will require an extraordinary grace of God and firm and self-sacrificing resolution on the part of men of good will and far-sighted vision. If such men are brought to perceive and appreciate the fascinating beauty of just social principles, they will be able by their influence to spread among the masses a conviction of the truly divine and spiritual origin of social life; and they will thus prepare the way for the re-awakening, the development, and the consolidation of those ethical conceptions without which the proudest achievement in the social sphere will be nothing but a Babel; its citizens may have walls in common, but they will speak different and conflicting tongues.

In order to collaborate in this work of spreading a *spiritual* influence in the world, now so deeply materialist, the Catholic moralist must proceed in two ways:

(*a*) He must try to formulate the essential and universal principles of the true spiritual basis of international morality.

(*b*) In the light of those principles, he must attempt to set out a collection of "historico-spiritual" judgements on the present world situation.

This chapter will thus be divided into two parts corresponding to these two modes of procedure.

ESSENTIAL PRINCIPLES

Contemporary popes have given their minds to the enunciation of these general principles of inter-State morality, Pius XII in particular having devoted many of his writings to this task. We shall therefore rely largely on these pontifical documents in setting out the essentials.

First principle: False nationalism must be eradicated from the minds of governments for the sake of the common good of all nations.

As its etymology shows, "nationalism" appeals to the idea of "the nation", so that to be clear about the excesses of nationalism which have to be avoided we must begin by seeing what is meant by "nation". Now in our first chapter we remarked that sociologists are today more or less agreed that a "nation" is an ethnic unit animated by the desire to live in common in order to pursue common ends. And we have also remarked that for there really to be a nation, this will to live in common for common ends must find expression in a minimum of outward and public signs, the commonest at the present time being for a nation to tend to constitute a sovereign State. This is not the only symptom of "nationalism", but it is in our times the most evident, and often also the most embarrassing; it is also at times a symptom of a people's dynamism.

This being so, when we speak of "false nationalism" we mean that certain perversions have been introduced into this "will to live in common for common ends" in the case of such and such a nation. History shows us that the actual forms taken by these perversions can be very different and even strange in the way they work. We can also see that they are the results not only of mistaken notions of the common ends to be pursued but also of "emotional complexes" which damage the very "will to live in common" itself.

To over-generalize, we can distinguish two "common denominators" of all false nationalisms.

1. A nation falls into a false nationalism when it succumbs to a sort of short-sightedness: it cannot see far enough to set its "national interests" in the context of the good of the whole community of man, the international common good, which alone makes it possible to conceive of and evaluate at their proper worth those more particular values.

2. A nation falls into false nationalism when such narrowness of outlook is joined with a generally aggressive attitude towards other nations—that is, towards the international community itself.

We must repeat that these general and constant characteristics of false nationalism are susceptible of very different political manifestations. We cannot here even sketch out the various ways in which in the past false nationalism has taken on political reality; we shall refer only to two of its present forms.

1. The nationalism of the western nations, which lately gathered to themselves overseas territories, during the period of colonial adventure.

2. The nationalism of the coloured peoples who are today being set free from colonial rule.

The form nationalism takes in the European "mother-countries" is a sort of survival from colonial days. We should frankly admit it: despite the pompous phraseology in which the activity of colonization was wrapped up, the whole process was marked, by and large, by short-sightedness and aggressiveness. What the European powers had in mind when they occupied overseas territories, if not exclusively, at least principally, was their own self-interest.

Although colonial occupation might theoretically, perhaps, have been justified in terms of the universal common good, on the grounds that it was necessary in order to ensure that there should be a general sharing of the material and cultural goods which are, as is quite rightly said, intended for all mankind, it was in fact motivated most often by a concern for the interests of the mother-country. When this fault was committed, it was not perhaps a "completely formal fault", for the national consciences of Europe were then in a sort of ethical fog. It has taken the development of international law in the last twenty years or so to show Western minds that international relations should be governed by a care for the common good of mankind taken as a whole.

All the same, when we look objectively at the methods of colonization, we cannot exonerate the Western nations from all blame, since those methods were undoubtedly influenced by a certain aggressiveness on the part of the white races towards those who are coloured.

Today, when all right-minded men are aware of the full horror of racialism and when for thinking men the fog which surrounded international law has largely dispersed, the desire to preserve the ties of allegiance between mother-country and colony is recognized as wrong and character-istic of excessive nationalism.

This first kind of false nationalism has produced an equal and opposite reaction in another kind of nationalism. Until recently, it was hardly possible, when speaking of certain coloured peoples, to talk of them as "peoples": black Africa, for example, was a medley of tribes and clans which the given sociological conditions on the spot opposed to one another; they were joined by no common language, and, since they had no writing, had no common his-torical tradition extending far into space or time. Now it is true that in many ways the laying down of frontiers on African soil by the colonial powers has not done away with but rather perpetuated this ethnic fragmentation. Each African territory gathered together in a haphazard way tribal and linguistic groups which were very numerous and often very small. Nevertheless, it appears that, out of the "peoples" the colonizer found occupying the land when he arrived, the European nations have by their arbitrary carving up of Africa produced "embryo" nations. Within the frontiers which were laid down, however haphazard they may have been once, there has been begotten in the native inhabitants, by the very presence of the colonizing power, "a desire to live in common for the common aim of emancipation".

Now, in 1961, this common desire of the new-born nations of Africa presents certain characteristics:

1. It is still in places somewhat superficial, and the old tribal rivalries are dormant rather than extinct.

2. It is still a little short-sighted, for the development of education is not sufficiently advanced for the ordinary African to be able to comprehend with any facility the scope and the values of the universal common good.

3. In certain cases at least, it includes a certain aggressiveness against the European powers. This is an almost necessary and instinctive reaction against the aggressiveness of the Europeans which the Africans feel, with good reason, they once suffered from.

It is enough to describe these characteristics, even in so summary a fashion, to see that the coloured peoples who are now becoming these new-born nations, if they allow themselves to develop without keeping a firm control on their will to live in common, will in their turn fall a prey to the temptations of nationalism.

They will not be tempted, as were and are the Europeans, by an obsolete and wrong colonial conservatism. They will be attracted to a local isolationism, to an "independence" which breaks with the solidarity demanded for the good of the community of nations.

Many of the troubles of our times can be explained by the meeting of these two nationalist tendencies, that towards an out-of-date colonialism and that towards independence and separatism.

This means that both the peoples who were once colonizers, and those who were colonized and are now becoming free peoples, must be on their guard against the temptations of false nationalism which draw each on in their respective, specific ways. Pius XI, in an allocution of December 24th, 1930, was already pointing this out:

> It will be very difficult, if not impossible, for peace to endure between peoples and nations if, instead of by a true and pure patriotism, they are governed by a raging and egoistical nationalism; that is, by hate and envy instead of by a mutual desire for good, by hostility and suspicion instead of by fraternal confidence, by open competition instead of by understanding and cooperation, by ambition for leadership and self-aggrandisement instead of by respect for and the protection of all the rights of men, be they the weakest and smallest.

Second principle: States and their governments should, for the sake of the international common good, faithfully observe pacts and treaties made in accordance with the law of nations.[1]

The necessity for such faithful observance was stressed by Pius XII in his encyclical *Summi Pontificatus* in October, 1939, in which he also had something important to say on the subject of past treaties: "With the passage of time and substantial alterations in circumstances, changes not foreseen and perhaps not foreseeable at the time the treaty was drawn up, the treaty as a whole or some of its clauses may become, or seem to have become, unjust, or impracticable,

[1] On the general conditions for the validity of a treaty between nations, see Birkenhead's *International Law*, Part II, Chapter IV.

or too difficult, for one or both parties." In such a case, the party which legitimately judges that such or such a treaty has in some unforeseen way become too onerous, must not straightway have recourse to force. On the contrary, the parties "must be ready to enter into discussions, in the event of delays occurring, or impediments, modifications, disputes—all those things which can occur not because of ill will but because of changes in circumstances and real conflicts of interest." And Pius XII stresses the necessity in such circumstances for genuine and sincere negotiation. In any case, he adds, the unilateral annulment of a promise given is never admissible.

All the same, we can say that an established international organization should normally, through certain of its organs, in many cases play the part of an arbitrator in this constant maintenance and administration of treaties.

Third principle: States of pluralist structure should avoid, for the sake of the international common good, oppressing national minorities gathered within their unity.

It is surely obvious that the revolt of this or that oppressed minority is not a purely internal affair: it might be contagious, or help might be asked for and obtained from outside. Pius XII was therefore surely right to declare, in his Christmas message of 1941, that for the sake of international peace, and not merely of peace within any nation, "there is no room in the operation of any new international organization founded on moral principles for the oppression, open or concealed, of cultural or linguistic minorities, for the shackling or restriction of their economic potentialities, or for the limitation or abolition of their natural fecundity."

But does this mean that any and every racial, cultural or linguistic minority existing within a pluralist State is always and unconditionally entitled to claim and to attempt to gain, even by force, its independence, and to set itself up as a sovereign State, even if it means a violent breaking away from that pluralist State?

That would surely be wrong. In deciding its attitude, such a minority should, it is true, consult its particular common good; but not *only* that particular good. It should also consult the larger common good of the pluralist State itself, of which it is, to begin with, a part, and from which it is considering seceding. And it must also consult the still wider common good of the whole community of mankind, since the repercussions of its particular actions will, at least indirectly, little by little affect that whole community.

Besides, Catholic international morality cannot unreservedly or without due precautions adopt the slogan so often nowadays lightly taken up: "every people has the right to govern its own affairs". This dictum can only be accepted if there is understood with it some such phrase as, "taking into account the needs of the pluralist State containing that people, and also the demands of the international common good". It is then the simple assertion that normally, and as a very general rule, a people forming a political minority in a pluralist State should be enabled to govern itself in a sovereign manner, if it is to be able fully to realize the social conditions of its own development and to satisfy in the best way possible the demands of the international common good; and this both for its own advantage and for that of the pluralist State to which it belongs, the life of which is conditioned by the general state of the international community.

Fourth principle: States and their governments should, for the sake of the international common good, rid themselves of all economic selfishness.

We shall return in Chapter VIII to the implications of this principle in the field of cooperation between developed and underdeveloped nations, but we must here stress the need for a general willingness to give economic help internationally. Pius XII laid this down as a *sine qua non* for the pursuit of the international common good: "There is no room in the operation of an international organization founded on moral principles for the narrow calculation of self-interest, which leads to the cornering of economic sources and materials in common use, with the result that the nations less favoured by nature must go without them." Pope John XXIII repeats and strengthens this teaching of his predecessors in the last part of his encyclical *Mater et Magistra* (Part III, Section 2).

Fifth principle: States and their governments should, for the sake of the international common good, base their relations on mutual trust and not on force and terror.

Benedict XV, in his message of August 1st, 1917, stressed that "the fundamental point should be that the moral force of right should replace the material force of arms," and Pius XII, twenty-four years later, gave expression to this same spiritual and moral concern in his Christmas message of 1941.

These very general principles of inter-State morality come together in a general requirement expressed by Pius XII in an address to the Sacred College on December 24th, 1945: "The present time imperiously demands the collaboration, the good will and the mutual trust of all nations. Motives of hate and vengeance, rivalry and antagonism, and dishonest and unfair competition, must be kept far removed from political and economic debates and decisions."

HISTORICO-SPIRITUAL JUDGEMENTS

To recall the minds of the nations' rulers to this fundamental spiritual outlook, the contemporary moralist cannot rest simply with the formulation in the abstract of the essential principles of the spiritual basis of international affairs. He must look at the present international situation and try, in the light of those principles, to make some judgements which we can call "historico-spiritual".

There is no room, in so short a book as this, to give a detailed analysis of the spiritual and intellectual bases of the present international situation. But we can, if we restrict ourselves to what is really essential, agree that the nations are faced with a general moral problem because of the division of the world into two opposing blocs: the East is dominated by Marxist powers, the West by the Western powers.

Moreover, we can broadly distinguish, since the war of 1939–45, two successive periods, which we may perhaps call the "Stalin" period and the "Khrushchev" period. The first was that of the "cold war"; the second is rather regarded, if we may use the words of the present Russian leader, as that of "peaceful coexistence". Consequently, the Catholic moralist had to make a historico-prudential judgement on the attitude of the nations during the cold war; and now he must make a historico-prudential judgement on their attitude in the period of peaceful coexistence. These judgements are, of course, far too general to dictate any policy properly so called; a great deal must be left to the politicians. But at least they seek to make clear the values which must not be sacrificed to events through illegitimate reactions. This is why, if only for the sake of example, it is profitable to recall what were the general directives inspired by Catholic international morality during the "cold war" of the "Stalin" period, and what they are now, in present circumstances, during the "Khrushchev" period of "peaceful coexistence".

THE "COLD WAR" PERIOD

In his Christmas message of 1947, Pius XII diagnosed the main symptoms of this period. "A vast wall," he said, "now stands between the two groups of East and West, so as to frustrate every effort to give back to the shattered family of mankind the benefits of a true peace." Following Pius XII, the Catholic moralist can perceive several causes of this tragic state of affairs.

1. First, a mutual distrust, which forced each camp back in on itself, put each on its guard against every action of the other side, and led each systematically to suspect the intentions of the other, to the point of mistrusting anything that seemed to suggest an attempt at understanding.

2. Because of this mutual suspicion, both blocs felt it necessary, "as a matter of elementary prudence", to use lying tactics, or at any rate tactics of insincerity, involving the use of the weapons of propaganda and psychological action.

3. This inclination towards insincerity was aggravated on the Communist side by the pressure of Marxist doctrine. This is what made their propaganda so dangerous, for it is the doctrine of totalitarian States. For them, there is no objective truth: a thing is true if it conforms to the interests of the party. For example, an event cannot be judged by and for itself; propaganda must look to see what use can be made of it for the advantage of the party, in order to increase its influence in the world. This leads to utter insecurity, for there are no limits to propaganda's powers of invention.

At Christmas, 1947, facing this situation squarely, Pius XII formulated the "historico-prudential" rule which the situation imposed on the two blocs if they were to return to the fundamentals of general inter-State morality. "No one today," he said, "to whatever social or political group or party he belongs, if he wants his own convictions and actions to count for something in the present or the future course of man's history, has the right to conceal his hand, to pretend to be what he is not, to rely on lying tactics, or to use constraint or threats to deny the good citizens of all countries the exercise of their proper freedom and their civil rights."

Such "historico-prudential" judgements as this have, we have said, a double reference, to absolute values on the one hand, and to historical, contingent events on the other. This judgement of the pope's has just this double reference.

The studies made by historians, diplomats, politicians and sociologists of war and peace are generally silent on this problem of insincerity. Even the best resolutions of the General Assembly of the United Nations, those proposing means of improving the prospects of peace, seem not to have dared to face this question. Yet how many must there have been at this period in the Assembly who knew in their hearts that such insincerity was a threat to peace, yet appeared resigned to suffer the ritual arguments of the totalitarian powers, attacking the other nations in terms so violent and insulting that not so long ago they would have constituted a *casus belli* themselves! Speaking or listening, it was all propaganda. No one believed in the truth of what was said, not even those who used the rostrum of the Assembly to stir up trouble or to retaliate. It was urgently necessary for men to recover themselves and protest, documents in hand, against lying accusations, and for all to understand that such a way of carrying on was a perpetual threat to peace.[2]

THE PERIOD OF "PEACEFUL COEXISTENCE"

After the death of Stalin and the advent of Khrushchev to power in Russia, the "cold war" was followed by the period of "peaceful coexistence". Khrushchev himself explained what he meant by that term in an article in the American review, *Foreign Affairs*, in October, 1959 (Vol. 38, No. 1):

What, then, is the policy of peaceful coexistence? In its simplest expression it signifies the repudiation of war as a

[2] Cf. Mgr Guerry: *L'Église et la communauté des peuples*, p. 56.

means of solving controversial issues. However, this does not cover the entire concept of peaceful coexistence. Apart from the commitment to non-aggression, it also presupposes an obligation on the part of all States to desist from violating each other's territorial integrity and sovereignty in any form and under any pretext whatsoever. The principle of peaceful coexistence signifies a renunciation of interference in the internal affairs of other countries with the object of altering their system of government or mode of life or for any other motives. The doctrine of peaceful coexistence also presupposes that political and economic relations between countries are to be based upon complete equality of the parties concerned and on mutual benefit.

This ideal, put forward by the president of the Council of Ministers of the U.S.S.R. and First Secretary of the Party, might appear morally very attractive to the nations of the world. But one Catholic moralist, Roger Heckel, S.J., in the *Revue de l'Action Populaire* for March, 1960, propounded the following historico-prudential judgement, taking his inspiration from Pius XII's Christmas message of 1954, which was devoted to the idea of coexistence.

Wise men [he said] will try to make the idea of coexistence an active force for peace by making it quite clear that it is in itself a far more constructive idea than war—*nothing is lost with peace, but all may be lost with war*; by bringing into the open the subversive dangers which threaten it—*there can be no coexistence in illusion*; by saving it from slipping, as it could easily and very naturally do, into an attitude of "peace at any price"—*there can be no coexistence in submission*; by preventing it from narrowing itself to a simple balance of fear— *there can be no coexistence in fear*; by freeing it from errors which might slow down, turn aside, or even reverse its progress towards peace—*there can be no coexistence in error*; and by guiding it firmly into the way of truth—*there can only be coexistence in truth*.

Behind the attractive picture of peaceful economic

competition painted by Khrushchev, peaceful coexistence as he himself sets it out still involves the permanent struggle of systems of life on the ideological level. The conflict which hides beneath the veil of "peaceful coexistence" involves, fundamentally, the conflict of two civilizations, the principles and forms of which are different, the official interpreters of which ceaselessly proclaim that they cannot be compatible, and each of which has shown, up to now, a surprising power of resistance to the other. Communism repudiates and ridicules the values of the West as the West lives them—or we might say, as the West betrays them in daily, observable life.

From all this it looks as though, under the banners of "peaceful coexistence", it is really, in many ways, the "cold war" which is still being carried on.

"Cold war" and "peaceful coexistence"—these are the contingent historical facts which the moralist has had to face in recent years, against which he has to set the eternal values in order to reach the historico-prudential judgements he needs to put forward in order to give a firm basis to the international morality of the nations. These historical facts, like all historical realities, are transitory. Doubtless tomorrow they will have yielded place to other facts themselves also marked by the same contingency, and these too will have to be judged by the moralist against the spiritual values whose witness and judge he is appointed to be. So his task can never be completed. But throughout the diversity of the historico-spiritual judgements he has to make on the passing and unexpected events of history, he must hold in the sight of all to his fundamental and unchanging duty, which is to see that politicians can and do return to the true and immutable principles of a spiritual morality, without which the common good of mankind is deprived of one of the conditions of its effective realization in the world.

CHAPTER VII

INTERNATIONAL DISPUTES

The contemporary Catholic moralist's views on the settlement of present international disputes are rooted in a whole tradition concerning war and peace left to him by past ages, a tradition drawn on by the moralists of the nineteenth century and the first half of the twentieth. And it is remarkable that the same tradition broadly inspired, at least implicitly, the great international conferences of The Hague in 1899 and 1907. The Geneva Conventions of August 12th, 1949, assume that its essential points are accepted; from this supposedly accepted philosophical basis those conventions draw the particular logical deductions and applications which the actual forms of warfare at that time suggested.

This chapter will be divided into two sections: the first will consist of a rapid and schematic summing-up of the form that traditional morality had assumed by the beginning of the twentieth century; in the second, after we have shown how and why present conditions have raised unexpected problems, we shall examine these new problems and try to discover the principles whereby they might be solved.

TRADITIONAL MORALITY

The traditional morality of peace and war grew up in the face of historical situations which were indeed extremely various. Nevertheless, it also grew in the context of a sociological whole which, seen at a distance, appeared to remain in many respects much the same through the differences of past ages, and which, taken by and large, seems to have had the following characteristics.

There certainly was a general feeling among men that, despite racial differences and political diversity, mankind constituted a true unity, and that therefore there was, over and above the interests and good of any political power, a common good of mankind. But until the nineteenth century this feeling remained nebulous and vague in the minds of the general public. In the minds of a good many "princes" and rulers of States it was almost non-existent. At the very most, some of them had a suspicion that the adverse political forces against which they found themselves ranged in practice had certain natural rights.

It is true that in the ages of medieval Christendom the various political units in Europe had some awareness that they were in some way related, because of the facts that their peoples belonged to the same Christian faith and to the Church, and that they owed a common allegiance to the emperor. But, on the one hand, these facts were only ever true of the peoples of Europe, and, on the other, these historical links were broken when medieval Christendom exploded into fragments at the time of the Renaissance. In any case, until very recent times, *there had never been established, or even suggested, a secular international organization.*

In the face of this general historical situation, Catholic moralists considered, at least implicitly, that war was an inevitable phenomenon. This conviction in their minds rested on their experience of the secular world. So far as they could see, from time to time and in this or that place, certain political powers would launch wars of aggression against rival powers, using their armies, which were generally made up of professional soldiers.

This inevitability of wars of aggression led them to draw the conclusion that there must be such a thing as a just war, the defensive war fought by the princes who were attacked or by the powers whose frontiers were violated by aggressors or whose rights were trampled underfoot.

This led naturally and progressively to the old moralists building up a theory of the just war, the principal propositions of which may be thus summarized.

TRADITIONAL MORALITY AND AGGRESSIVE WAR

A war in which one political power initiated hostilities against another, either to satisfy a selfish ambition or to assert its own rights over the other's, without first using all the diplomatic and peaceful means at its disposal, was in itself an unjust war. It was immoral.

This principle of traditional morality was clearly sound when the power in question was realizing a purely selfish ambition, and when, therefore, the act of war was committed in an unjust cause. It was also clearly sound when, even though the cause was just, the attacking power had not first exhausted all peaceful means of removing the wrong done to it, for then that power would be unleashing the terrible evils which accompany war without good reason.

But theologians tended to absolve a State which attacked first, if it intended by attacking to ensure the victory of an undeniable right, after fruitless recourse to all possible means of peaceful settlement. Nevertheless, they insisted that the importance of the cause should be sufficient to justify the evils produced by war, and that the other conditions for a just war should be satisfied.

TRADITIONAL MORALITY AND DEFENSIVE WAR

A defensive war by which a power, unjustly attacked, tried to defend the rights of its people was regarded by the old moralists, in the international situation we have described, as a just war, at least so far as its cause was concerned.

Obviously, as we shall see in a moment, for a defensive war to be fully justified it had to fulfil other conditions also. But, supposing those conditions satisfied, it was obvious that in the international situation of that time, when there was no established international process for effectively ensuring the victory of right over unjust aggression, if all other diplomatic and judicial means had been tried in vain, the only alternative left to the power attacked was to defend itself against injustice. So a defensive war waged by a State against the unjust aggression of another was seen, theoretically at least, as an act of justice—the only such act internationally possible—intended to maintain the law or to re-establish it.

TRADITIONAL MORALITY AND THE CONDITIONS OF A JUST WAR

Nonetheless, traditional Catholic morality gradually worked out more and more clearly certain conditions which had to be satisfied, all together at the same time, if even a defensive war was to be fully justified. They can be briefly summarized in these five points.

1. The cause served by such a war had to be manifestly just.

2. The intentions of those fighting such a war had to remain right intentions throughout hostilities: that is, they should never be animated by a desire for vengeance, but by concern for the re-establishment of justice.

3. It was essential that those fighting such a war should, before they began fighting, have exhausted all peaceful means of settlement open to them which were, humanly speaking, possible.

4. The methods of warfare had to be just; that is, they had to correspond to the rules of law fixed by the established custom of the nations or, later, by signed international agreements.

5. It was necessary that the power entering on such a war had a reasonable chance of succeeding, and that the good anticipated from final victory was, judging all things carefully and wisely, proportionate both to the evils war would bring in its train and also to the serious consequences that would follow from it once peace was re-established.

TRADITIONAL MORALITY AND THE TREATMENT OF PRISONERS, NON-BELLIGERENTS, OPEN CITIES AND HOSTAGES

These value-judgements of traditional morality on the initiation and conduct of hostilities were backed up by rules on the treatment of prisoners, of non-combatants, of open cities and of hostages.

Prisoners-of-war

It has to be admitted that the oldest moralists were not at all gentle towards prisoners-of-war. Francisco de Vitoria himself still thought "that it would, properly speaking, be no violation of justice if, *in a just war*, guilty prisoners were put to death".[1]

But there was a gradual refinement of the moral conscience on this point. The final judgement of traditional morality was that combatants who respected the laws of war were not to be held personally responsible, and that prisoners-of-war had an unquestioned right to live.

Non-belligerents

In the situation of their time, when all armies consisted of professional soldiers, the old moralists had no difficulty in

---

[1] Vitoria, *De jure belli*, No. 49.

clearly distinguishing combatants and non-combatants. This being so, without straying beyond the bounds of justice those who made war could not, in principle, use violence against the inhabitants of the enemy's country who took no active part in the war. They could not, therefore, attack non-belligerents. However, if those who fought justly could not directly and intentionally attack the lives of the peaceful inhabitants of the enemy's country, they were nevertheless not forbidden to carry out operations in the course of battle which must necessarily involve the loss of innocent lives. How did the moralists justify this? This loss of non-combatant lives, they said, was not directly willed, it was simply tolerated as a secondary effect, inevitably bound up with the legitimate end pursued by the just belligerent. So they admitted that the just belligerent might open fire on expressly military objectives even if in so doing he might hit—without deliberately intending to—private houses, schools or hospitals, and kill non-combatants.

Open cities

At the time we are considering, traditional moralists could easily distinguish fortified places and open cities. They condemned the bombardment of open cities. Since, they thought, such cities made no resistance to occupation by the just belligerent, he would be guilty of useless cruelty if he bombarded "open cities" in which the non-belligerent population would be the victims.

Hostages

Belligerents who invaded or occupied an enemy territory often took hostages, who guaranteed with their lives the safety of the invading or occupying troops. Such a practice, deriving from barbaric custom, making the innocent pay for the guilty, seemed to traditional moralists to be incompatible with the demands of right, and in their eyes the killing of hostages for the hostile acts of third parties clearly constituted a crime.

Moreover, it seemed to them equally criminal to place hostages on military objectives particularly exposed to the enemy's fire.

TRADITIONAL MORALITY AND THE RIGHTS AND DUTIES OF OCCUPYING POWERS

Traditional morality also laid down certain broad principles concerning the rights and duties of occupying powers in the land invaded and those of the occupied powers. These principles in broad outline were laid down in The Hague Conferences of 1899 and 1907, and Cardinal Mercier, in his famous pastoral letter of Christmas, 1914, when the Germans were overrunning Belgium, recalled their essential points, which were summed up in 1948 in the Code of Malines in this way:

> The inhabitants of a country occupied by an unjust aggressor still owe allegiance to the legal government of their country. To the occupying power they owe only an exterior submission which does not involve their loyalty. As Cardinal Mercier wrote, "the acts of public administration of the occupying power would in themselves have no force, but the legitimate authority of the legal government is held tacitly to ratify those acts which are justified by the general interest, and from this ratification alone comes all their juridical force".
>
> The occupying power must try to re-establish and to guarantee, as far as is possible, public order and public life, by respecting, unless absolutely prevented from so doing, the laws in force in the country. Its inhabitants cannot be forced to take part in operations of war directed against their own country. The honour and rights of families, and the lives of individuals, their religious beliefs and freedom of worship must be respected. Private property cannot be confiscated.

Should the occupying power, in place of the legal government, levy taxes, they must be allocated for their usual uses. Should other taxes be exacted, they must only be used for the needs of the army or for the administration of the occupied territory. No collective fine should be levied against the whole population because of the acts of individuals for which the people as a whole cannot be considered responsible. Requisitions in kind and services cannot be demanded except as just compensation.

The occupying power has a provisional title to the ownership of the goods of the enemy State located in the invaded territory. In principle, it can only perform acts of administration. But natural resources useful for the prosecution of the war may nevertheless be seized by the occupying army, even if they belong to private persons. Goods held in common, and those belonging to institutions devoted to worship, to works of charity, or to the arts or sciences, even if they belong to the State, should be treated as private property.

The State which is the victim of unjust aggression and forced to abandon to an invader the whole or part of its territory, preserves the right to organize secret forces which can support, within the country, the action of armies of liberation.

Even if no initiative is taken by the legal authority, active resistance by the occupied people is still justified as the exercise of the legitimate right of self-defence against immoral acts of the occupying power in violation of the formal rules of the law of nations: deportation, forced labour for the enemy's advantage, forced conscription in the enemy's army, etc. But even then, resistance should not be anarchic, but should be conducted with discipline and with respect for the requirements of international morality.

TRADITIONAL MORALITY AND THE VICTOR IN A JUST WAR

Traditional morality considered the problem of the conditions which the victor in a just war should impose on an enemy who admits himself defeated. Suarez summed those conditions up as follows:

1. The restitution of all goods unjustly seized by the enemy.

2. The repayment of all expenses incurred because of his injustice.

3. Some punishment for the fault committed; for in war there is room for retributive justice alongside commutative justice.

4. All claims necessary for the preservation and defence of peace; for the principal object of a just war is precisely the laying of the foundations of a lasting peace.[2]

While recognizing that the victor in a just war had the right to punish the guilty, traditional theologians, especially Suarez and Vitoria, nevertheless attached to that right certain reservations:

1. A certain good faith may sometimes excuse a belligerent who has, objectively, no just cause for making war. In such a case he should not be punished for a fault of which he is not formally guilty.[3]

2. The general common good may sometimes suggest a relaxation of the effects of retributive justice.[4]

These teachings of traditional morality were repeated by Pius XII in his Christmas message of 1944:

It is, humanly speaking, understandable, and perhaps inevitable in practice, that certain peoples, whose governments—and perhaps even themselves, in part—can be held responsible for the war, should for some time have to suffer strict measures of security until the bonds of mutual confi-

2 Suarez, *De tripl. virt. theol.*, III, Disp. XIII, Sect. VII, No. 5.
3 Vitoria, *De jure belli*, No. 59.
4 Suarez, *loc. cit.*, Sect. VII, No. 3.

dence so violently broken are gradually renewed. Nevertheless, even these peoples must be given the firm hope that, in
proportion as they cooperate loyally and effectively in the
future work of restoration, they will be able to be associated,
just like other nations, with the same consideration and with
the same rights, in the great community of nations. To refuse
them this hope would be the opposite of wise foresight.

TRADITIONAL MORALITY AND THE VICTOR IN AN UNJUST WAR

In the case when an unjust belligerent is victor, traditional
morality is extremely firm in its judgement. The Code of
Malines faithfully reproduced that judgement:

> Of itself, a treaty dictated by a victorious unjust belligerent
> is null and void: the force which imposes it does not create a
> right. The defeated nation is, however, bound to conform to it,
> not out of respect for the right of the victor, for no such right
> exists, but in the interests of its own subjects and of the inter-
> national community, which it is bound to spare the horrors of
> another war.
>
> From the radical nullity of the rights arrogated to himself
> by the unjust conqueror, it follows that should a later con-
> flict arise, not provoked by the defeated, in which the previous
> victor is engaged, the defeated may assert his rights and
> demand the restitution of the goods and territories of which he
> has been unjustly despoiled.

Such, in broad outline, are the conclusions reached on
the just war by traditional morality, conclusions worked
out, we may repeat, in the context of past historical situations.

NEW PROBLEMS AND THE REASONS FOR THEM

If the moralist is today faced with new problems, it is
because the general international situation in our time is no
longer exactly similar to what it was in the past. The

essential newness of the present situation can be analysed into the following points:

1. Nowhere today, so to say, are there professional armies properly so called; most great powers use the method of general conscription. In case of war, all the nation's means are at the disposal of the armed forces. In short, we live in the age of armed nations, a state of things which has led in recent years to a general "armaments race".

2. Modern war has become "total war". In time of war, all the nation's resources are used for the service of the armed forces. A workman in a factory far from the scene of battle has come to be a "combatant" in the same way as a soldier "at the front", simply because in some way his work strengthens the war potential of his country. So the classical distinction between combatants and non-combatants has to a large extent become vague and indefinable.

3. In the same way, the distinction between "open cities" and "fortified places" no longer has much meaning. An urban agglomeration including an important station, a junction of many roads, and a collection of factories working for the armed forces, is as much or more a military objective than a city surrounded by ramparts.

4. The means now usable in war have changed in nature, by changing in size. The atomic bomb marks a real historical change. So too do the chemical and bacteriological methods now usable. From all the evidence we now have, an "A.B.C. war" (atomic, bacteriological, chemical) would, if launched on a world-wide scale, threaten the survival of humanity as a whole.

5. An important conflict is much more difficult to confine as a "local war" than it used to be. Because of the development of communications between peoples, it runs the real risk of quickly becoming a global conflict. It necessarily involves, much more than heretofore, not only the common

good of the nations actually fighting, but the common good of all humanity.

6. The consequences, psychological, social, cultural, economic and spiritual, of a world war are now infinitely more profound and more serious than those of the limited conflicts of times past.

7. A new and unforeseen form of war has appeared: "subversive and revolutionary" war. In such a war, it is no longer a matter of organized forces gathered into coherent fighting bodies facing one another, but of "commandos" scattered over a wide territory, or of whole peoples saturated in propaganda. The manipulation of the thoughts of men, "psychological warfare", plays as decisive a rôle in such a war as material arms. It is not so much a matter of winning a battle as of depriving the established power in the enemy's territory of its control, of paralysing its action, of gaining power by the psychological control of the population through a well-defined ideology.

8. Yet while in the past, in the age of traditional morality, there was no secular organization of States, there is today such an international organization, however imperfect, among the aims of which are precisely the assurance of security and the prevention of armed conflicts by finding peaceful and juridical solutions to the disagreements which arise between nations.

9. Thanks to the development of historical studies and disciplines, past wars are now considered with more penetration, more competence and more critical acumen than ever before. War has almost never been what the old theologians imagined that it was. In fact, only very rarely can it be seen as the exercise of a judicial or retributive function; belligerents have generally faced one another not as just men and guilty, but as competitors. A conflict arises between them; they have recourse to force to settle it: and that is all. War has never been anything more than a

simple means of removing an opponent. The community of nations has always admitted, in a completely practical way, that the victor has legally won: the treaty of peace which ended a war became law. Essentially, war has never been anything but an effective means of altering the legal relations between nations.

In the view of contemporary historians, therefore, the old theologians' theory of the "just war" has become to a large extent only a theoretical abstraction, very fine, no doubt, in the abstract, but almost always bearing no relation to historical reality.

With such vast changes in the actual situation facing the moralist, the problem of war and peace has given rise to unforeseen questions. We shall now examine from the moralist's point of view some of the major questions that have arisen.

First question: What is the position of contemporary international morality with regard to the present international climate, which still makes room for war as a normal means of settling certain international conflicts?

In so far as the present international climate still leaves room for war as a means of settling international disputes, the Catholic moralist must now show himself firm and severe in his disapproval. He judges recourse to war as irrational and spiritually shocking.

It is irrational, for the rules of war are based on an implicit principle which, strictly speaking, is absurd. This principle can be formulated thus: the victor shall be the one who was initially in the right, and he shall have the legitimate right to fix whatever peace terms he wishes. Now there is no *a priori* guarantee either that the victor will indeed be the one who was in the right, or that the terms of peace he dictates once he has won will be really reasonable and right. On the contrary, history shows that it was often the pirates who won, and that the victors, when it came to dictating peace terms, were often swayed more by passion than by justice and equity.

It is spiritually shocking because, taken in itself, a human situation in which men fight against one another is one in which the Gospel ideal is betrayed: "Love one another."

Moreover, even when it is finished, a war leaves terrible consequences behind it, not only material destruction, but numberless economic, social, moral and spiritual disorders.

And lastly, from the point of view of the Church, war creates a singularly paradoxical situation: within Catholic Christendom itself, her children are divided into opposing camps, and kill one another.

Because of all this, the moralist today must try by every means in his power to eliminate war, as far as possible, from the field of international relations, rather than simply seeking to make as just as possible wars whose inevitability is taken for granted.

Second question: What does the contemporary Catholic moralist think of theories of "non-violence"?

This question is asked because there are those who believe that the only way for a State today to work for the creation of truly peaceful international relations is for it to practise absolute and unconditional non-violence. To this, the Catholic moralist cannot reply so unequivocally.

It would be an illusion to think that we shall be able here on earth to attain to a real brotherhood of nations—which is how men ought to live—without frequently having to face violent and unrestricted injustice and put it down. Because Christianity has no illusions about the state of man, such as it is now, whether we like it or not, however high the ideal set before us by the Gospel, Christianity cannot be confused with any doctrine of absolute and unconditional non-violence.

This has important consequences, firmly insisted upon by Pius XII in his Christmas messages of 1948 and 1956. Beyond any doubt, a government which is responsible for the life of its people and for certain values which are necessary for the safety of its people, must work with others for the establishment of a state of international affairs in which aggression becomes impossible. But inasmuch as that state of international affairs does not yet fully exist, a contemporary government's responsibilities for its subjects oblige it to provide effectively against unjust aggression, which is still possible, and perhaps in the event to fight against such aggression, which would threaten the persons and the values under its protection. A defensive war, provided that it satisfied the traditional conditions for a just war, could still today be quite in accord with the requirements of morality, properly understood. So the Catholic moralist cannot require contemporary States to practise absolute and unconditional non-violence in a world of armed nations in which the temptation to aggression is not yet dead.

Third question: Has the just war now disappeared from the international scene?

This question, related to the preceding one, has been raised by certain contemporary theologians. Some of them have been led to hold that in the present world situation no war, even a defensive war against an unjust aggressor, can possibly be just. Cardinal Ottaviani, for example, has written: *Bellum est omnino interdicendum.*[5]

The arguments alleged in favour of such a position can be reduced essentially to two.

1. There does now exist a secular international organization. Hence, the use of force which is necessary to oppose

---

[5] *Institutiones juris publici ecclesiatici*, 3rd edn, Marietti, Turin, vol. 1, p. 151, No. 86.

aggression ought, in a community of nations which has thus grown up, to be reserved to the international police of that organization.

2. The nature of war itself has completely changed. It has become a vast technique of destruction, more and more effective, and less and less able to distinguish those it strikes. The result is that the moralist is faced by a double perplexity. He has always believed that the evils caused by war could and should be less than the advantages hoped for from it; but is this still possible, with modern wars? He has also always believed that non-belligerents should not be attacked (except accidentally, without it being directly willed); is this discrimination between belligerents and non-belligerents still possible? Must one not therefore say that modern war, even defensive war, is of its very nature contrary to the requirements of morality and therefore to be absolutely condemned?

Yet it seems too much to hold that today even a defensive war cannot be a just war. Pius XII was much more moderate, as can be seen from his Christmas message of 1948, his address to the Sixth Congress of Penal Lawyers on October 3rd, 1953, and his address to the Sixteenth Congress of Military Doctors on October 19th, 1953.

> The community of nations [Pius XII said on October 3rd, 1953] still has to reckon with criminals with no conscience who do not scruple to launch total war in order to further their own ambitions. That is why, if the rest of the nations of the world want to protect their existence and their most precious possessions, and if they do not want to give free rein to international wrongdoers, they have no choice but to prepare for the day when they might have to defend themselves. *Even today*, this right to hold oneself ready to defend oneself cannot be denied to any nation.

It has been rightly pointed out by others that the two arguments, on which those rely who say that a just defensive war is impossible, have neither the force nor the certitude, nor the obviousness, that they are credited with.

1. We have spoken in an earlier chapter of the powerlessness of the existing international organization to provide an effective international police force, or to enforce its decisions by effective sanctions. What we have said shows clearly enough that this weakness of the international organization still leaves it to individual States to assume the responsibility for the defence of their own rights in this or that particular case.

2. It seems an act of presumption to declare *a priori* that there cannot now or in future be any proportion between the evils which result from a defensive war and the good human causes one might be compelled to defend whatever the cost in particular cases. Nevertheless, for a defensive war to be fully just, in every respect, it must still conform to the rules for a just war laid down by traditional morality, which we have described and which were stated once again in the Geneva Convention of August 12th, 1949.

This raises another question which troubles many contemporary minds.

Fourth question: In the case of a defensive war undertaken for a just cause, does the Catholic moralist recognize the right of the just belligerent to use atomic weapons, and bacteriological and chemical warfare?

This problem was dealt with on several different occasions by Pius XII, and the views expressed by him imply the solutions of all the crises of conscience which statesmen might in practice have to face on the subject of an "A.B.C. war". They can be summed up in this way.

1. As we shall see later when we deal with disarmament, it is altogether desirable that all nations shall by common agreement renounce the use of these methods of warfare. To this end, they must at once give up the testing of nuclear

weapons, and those who possess such weapons must all simultaneously destroy their stocks. In both these cases there must be an effective international control.

2. In so far as we have not yet achieved this situation, the question of the legality or illegality of an "A.B.C. war" can and should be treated with reference to the traditional principles of theology on the just war, which are still valid at this time. Consequently, the use of such methods of warfare would be, in itself, morally tolerable in certain cases of legitimate self-defence, if it should prove necessary in the present state of international affairs, when there exists no agreement on simultaneous, controlled and guaranteed nuclear disarmament.

3. However, granted the terrible consequences of the use of atomic weapons, the injustice against which such means of defence would be used, if no other means could stop it, must be of such gravity that it threatens to destroy the very foundations of international order itself.

4. There is, however, a point beyond which conditional toleration of the use of such weapons could not logically go; nor should it ever under any circumstances. In the event of the harmful effects of the means envisaged passing completely beyond the control of man, no reason of legitimate defence or safeguard against any injustice, however grave, could be sufficient to justify their use. The good expected to accrue from their use could not constitute a reason proportionate to the evils which would be voluntarily, if indirectly, accepted. "The use of means which were completely uncontrollable in their annihilating effects must therefore be rejected as immoral; it could never be allowed for any cause" (Address of Pius XII, September 30th, 1954).

Fifth question: Has a belligerent, even supposing he is engaged in a just war, the right to use torture to discover the enemy's plans?

This question has interested and troubled many men's minds in recent years, especially during the fighting in Algeria. But the Catholic moralist's answer is unhesitating, and was in fact stated by the Cardinals and Archbishops of France during that war, in October, 1960:

Whichever side perpetrates them, acts of terrorism, outrages against the human person, *violent methods of obtaining information*, summary executions, and measures of reprisal against innocent persons are all condemned by God. [And they gave the general reason for this condemnation:] Even to assure the victory of legitimate right and the triumph of a cause believed to be just, no one can ever be allowed to have recourse to means which are intrinsically wrong, the use of which, by degrading the consciences of men, can have no other certain effect than continually to push further away the hour of peace. We must add that such actions make difficult the exercise of responsible command, and undermine, in the minds of subordinates, the legitimacy of authority.

Some may think it odd that the Catholic moralist, who allows that men may be killed in a just war, cannot admit that they can be tortured. But this only arises because of a radical misunderstanding. Procedures which aim to annihilate a man's freedom and ability to think, in order to make him speak, are "intrinsically wrong". In other words, it cannot ever be permissible to reduce a man, who because he is a man thinks and speaks, to the condition of a dog who barks. That is worse than shooting a man; it is not even commensurate. For to die is human: a man faced with death is still a man; he is capable of "taking in" the event of his death, which is forced upon him from without; he can freely give it a meaning and a point; he can make it, for example, a protest or a witness. But on the other hand, a man under torture is no longer a man, but is reduced purely and simply to the condition of an animal. No one ever has the right—even if some good may result—to reduce a man to that state, not even if it is true that the normal state of man includes some part which is animal and purely reflex, underlying his powers of reflective thought and his freedom.

Sixth question: If an enemy, during a subversive and revolutionary war, systematically uses psychological warfare, is it legitimate to use the same methods against him in order to neutralize his efforts?

This question also has aroused a great deal of attention in recent years. The theory of psychological warfare has been inspired by the writings of Mao Tse Tung, and is based on what seems broadly to be an irrefutable fact of collective psychology. There are in man—especially in man "in the mass"—areas of "mental reflexes". His opinions are more made up of these mental reflexes than of personal, thought-out beliefs. Now there are techniques of mass psychology; there are methods, effective under certain conditions, for creating, controlling and systematically exploiting "mental conditioned reflexes", methods every crowd, every mass is susceptible to, simply because of human psychology.

Now, relying on this scientific fact of psychology, certain military theorists have defined the proper rôle of psychological warfare in a subversive war in these terms:

1. The objectives which the armed forces are to pursue or defend should be clearly defined, since it is an essential condition of the morale of the troops and of the nation at war that they be precisely known.

2. These objectives should be expressed in simple, clear and short phrases.

3. There should be established a corps of instructors and propagandists whose duty it would be to instil these phrases into the minds not only of the troops but also of the civilian population.

4. This corps should be provided with the right propaganda techniques; that is, the techniques for creating

and exploiting the conditioned reflexes of the masses—techniques which are effective when used on any mass, particularly one mobilized for war.

5. A systematic and powerful effort should be made to discover the enemy's objectives, the slogans in which those objectives have been "condensed", and the methods used to create "conditioned reflexes" in the minds of the enemy's people and to exploit them systematically.

6. For this purpose intelligence services should be created.

7. Ideologies must be answered with ideologies, slogans with slogans, without scruple, for it is only a matter of turning against an enemy with whom one is at war the weapons he himself is using.

The Catholic moralist has to be very careful in deciding what his attitude is towards a just belligerent who repays his enemy in his own coin by using the same methods. Certainly we must not forget, because of the abuses to which such methods are susceptible, that there can be a certain legitimate use of propaganda. In particular, it seems that we ought not to deny to an army charged by a legitimate government with the winning of a subversive and revolutionary war, any use at all of psychological warfare. No one, in fact, will deny that one has the right to fight against the enemy's propaganda, which might exert a decisive influence on the issue of the struggle.

However, the following remarks may be made about this situation:

1. A situation dominated, in one sense or another, by the systematic and massive exploitation of the conditioned reflexes of the mass is in itself abnormal, humanly and spiritually. The same must be said about it as is said about war, even just war: it is abhorrent. For such a situation tends to develop in man what is inhuman, the mental reflexes, instead of what is human, reflective thought.

2. The systematic exploitation of the conditioned mental reflexes of the masses is therefore to be classified among means of violence, and the language of the military theorists is not mistaken when they speak of psychological "warfare". It should follow, then, that one can apply to the techniques of psychological warfare the general rules which are applicable to means of violence used in any just war:

(a) Before violent means of defence are used, there must be no doubt that the non-violent means of resolving the dispute are insufficient to ensure effective and legitimate defence.

(b) The use of such means must be restricted to the necessary minimum.

(c) It would be desirable—though it may in many cases seem no more than a pious hope—that an agreement should be reached on reciprocal, controlled and guaranteed "disarmament" in this field of psychological weapons. The morality of "psychological warfare" is no different from that of other forms of war.

3. The technicians of the "psychological services" must admit that the methods of exploiting systematically the conditioned reflexes of the masses can be used in the service of any cause whatever. There is therefore no avoiding the essential question of the true value of the cause in whose service they are to be used.

4. The "persuaders" must constantly ask themselves whether they are not themselves, more or less unconsciously, the playthings of the conditioned mental reflexes of the specialized crowd to which they belong. Since the normal disciplines of war tend to develop, of necessity, and at least among the lower ranks, reflex action, and to abolish, at least momentarily, reflective and thought-inspired action, every serviceman is thus threatened—because of the discipline under which he lives and must live on the battlefield—

with the chance that he may himself become the prey of unconscious mental reflexes produced by constant "blind obedience".

5. The "persuaders" should also remember the story of the sorcerer's apprentice and be aware of the slippery slope that leads from a morally tolerable use of counter-propaganda to a "management of minds" that would deserve the condemnations pronounced by Pius XII against the Chinese Communists' frightening "brain-washing".

6. This being so, the systematic exploitation of the conditioned reflexes of the masses, even when its use in a just war is to some extent justifiable, must leave plenty of room for the complementary methods which appeal to reflective thinking and "conversion by consent".

7. The right practice of the true intellectual disciplines is the normal condition of interior health. Now every educative discipline includes some "psychological action". The Church herself, in that infinite respect for man which characterizes her pedagogy, provides the "persuaders" with the exact limits they should observe. She is not unaware of the lower regions of the human mind, and knows how to use in her work of education the habits and reflexes with which the awakening of the child begins. This she does to help man's freedom to grow, never to stifle it. That is why she addresses herself much more to the intellect and the will than to the mechanisms of instinct. She knows that faith can only be the free and thoughtful adherence of a baptized soul, led by the grace of the Spirit which dwells in it from the moment of its baptism. Those who, in their apostolate, misunderstand this need for thought and for freedom, demanded by true faith, betray both man and the Church.

We could wish, therefore, that those who seek to establish or to reestablish by psychological action among a population the sense of certain natural values which they wish to defend in war, should be inspired by the example given them by the Church when she seeks to establish within herself and in her own field the sense of supernatural values.

Seventh question: What does the Catholic moralist think of the present general situation, in which most of the great nations practise some form of compulsory military service?

He cannot but judge such a situation wicked, unfortunate and deplorable. Writing for Benedict XV to Lloyd George, the British Prime Minister, Cardinal Gasparri wrote on September 28th, 1917: "Compulsory military service has been for more than a century the real cause of countless evils." In saying this, he was only repeating what Leo XIII had already said in his encyclical *Praeclara gratulationis*, of June 20th, 1894. In a letter to Pius IX, the Fathers of the Vatican Council of 1870 described the tragic effects they thought followed from compulsory military service: "The present state of the world is absolutely intolerable, because of the existence of vast armies, which are permanent and recruited by conscription. The peoples of the world groan under the burden of taxation. . . . As a result, there is less to distribute to the poor, commerce is paralysed, the conscience of man is either completely misled and perverted or shamefully wounded, and because of all this many souls are lost."

Besides these economic and spiritual ills, Benedict XV and, in his name, Cardinal Gasparri, justly remarked that this state of affairs was historically at the root of the terrible "armaments race". They therefore hoped that the nations would reach a common agreement to dispense with compulsory military service.

Eighth question: Is the Catholic moralist in favour of disarmament?

All that we have just written shows that the Catholic

moralist longs for the disarmament of all nations. On the other hand, what we have written above about non-violence also shows that it would be fanciful and dangerous to hope to achieve it by means of unilateral disarmament. In fact, the Catholic moralist envisages a disarmament which is:

(1) progressive,
(2) general and simultaneous,
(3) reached by mutual agreement,
(4) controlled,
(5) and, as far as possible, guaranteed by the sanctions of an international authority.

In the letter already quoted, Cardinal Gasparri wrote, as far back as 1917:

> The Holy Father believes that the only practicable and easily realizable means of achieving a reciprocal and simultaneous disarmament would be for an agreement to be reached by all civilized nations, neutrals included, on the simultaneous and reciprocal cessation of compulsory military service, and for a judicial court to be established to settle international disputes, provided with sanctions such as the isolation or general boycotting of any nation which tried to reestablish compulsory military service, or which refused to bring its international disputes before the court or to accept its decisions.

Pius XII constantly held and expressed the same views as Benedict XV. Four months after the beginning of the Second World War, considering the conditions of a real return to peace, Pius XII wrote in his Christmas message of 1939:

> In order that the peace shall be a true and lasting one, the nations must be set free from the terrible bondage of the armaments race, and from the danger that material forces may, instead of being a guarantee of right, become on the contrary a tyrannical instrument of its violation. Peace terms which do not give fundamental importance to a disarmament mutually agreed upon, organic and progressive, both in the

practical and in the spiritual order, and which are not faithfully adhered to, will eventually suffer the effects of their instability and lack of firmness.

Pius XII returned to the same theme in his Christmas messages of 1941, 1951 and 1954, and in 1955 he applied his teachings to nuclear weapons, asking for an agreement among the nations to renounce the testing of atomic bombs and their use in war. He also asked for a general control of disarmament.

To this last idea he returned in 1956, in his Christmas message, believing that it was only within the framework of an international organization such as the United Nations that such a control could effectively work:

> We should like to see the authority of the United Nations Organization strengthened, especially in order to achieve general disarmament, which is so close to our heart, and of which we have spoken so often. In fact, it is only within the framework of an organization such as U.N.O. that the undertaking of each nation to reduce its armaments and especially to give up the production and use of certain kinds of weapons could be given in common concord and made into a strict obligation in international law. In the same way, only the United Nations is at present in a position to demand the observance of such an agreement, by assuring the effective control of the armaments of each and every nation without exception.

But it is clear to the Catholic moralist that, whatever legal and institutional steps are taken to achieve material disarmament, they will be in vain if they are not preceded or accompanied by a spiritual disarmament. As Pius XII said in 1951: "Disarmament, that is, the simultaneous and reciprocal reduction of armaments, which we have always desired and appealed for, is no solid guarantee of a lasting peace if it is not accompanied by the abolition of the weapons of hate and greed and the limitless desire for prestige."

To support their teaching on disarmament, it is noticeable that besides arguments drawn from the Gospel teaching, the popes have advanced reasons in the natural, human and social order: the intolerable burden of taxation borne by the peoples of nations involved in the armaments race; the terrible death-dealing power of modern weapons and the horrifying devastation they have produced and are increasingly capable of producing; the agitation caused among the nations by the development and making of new weapons, and the fear and anguish they cause among peoples who hate and detest them; and the certainty that armaments, far from guaranteeing peace, only imperil it. Such arguments are worthy of deep consideration, and should be fervently welcomed.

To set out the views of the Catholic moralist on disarmament fully would necessitate, besides the statement of principles we have attempted here, an analysis of the negotiations which have followed one another, first on the Disarmament Commission and then, since 1955, at "summit" conferences; an analysis of the reasons why all these talks have up to now broken down without result; and a statement of the "historico-prudential" judgements implied in these breakdowns. But we have set out in broad outline the opinions of the Catholic moralist on present international disputes, and the principles involved.

CHAPTER VIII

FRATERNAL AID
AMONG THE NATIONS

In the Catholic moralist's view, it would be wrong to imagine that the ideal of an international community, to
which the nations must aspire for the reasons we have
given, only required of them the elimination of war, or at
any rate the ethical conduct of any wars breaking out among
them. This would imply only a negative idea of the international common good.[1] In fact, this international common
good prescribes a positive task: the nations must give
fraternal aid to one another.

The general duty of inter-State assistance certainly
includes obligations among the "developed" nations to one
another, for they are by no means all equally developed.
For example, Spain today has a general standard of living
which is lower than that of the rest of western Europe. It
must also be said that States which are relatively "modern-

---

[1] Certainly it has until very recently been a failing of Catholic writings
on international morality that they have made too brief a mention of
the positive duty of giving international aid. Taparelli d'Azeglio, for
example, when he deals with goodwill between nations, with regard to
material and moral goods, gives only a few brief lines to the obligation
which lies on all nations to help one another to obtain the various
goods, while the rules for the just war occupy eighteen pages of his
work. In the same way, the Code of International Morality of Malines,
in its 1948 edition, only has one or two references to the duty of rich
States to help the poor nations.

ized "—such as those of the Common Market—may unite for the benefit of their own regional areas of underdevelopment. For example, France should help to do something about southern Italy. Within the E.E.C., indeed, such cooperation is taking place.

But in view of the general world situation, that is not the most important aspect of this question. The point was made very strongly by John XXIII in his encyclical *Mater et magistra*: "Probably the most difficult problem today concerns the relationship between political communities that are economically advanced and those in the process of development."

THE GENERAL SITUATION

Humanity today has become more and more aware of this problem because of the increasingly precise comparisons now made of the differing standards of living in the world.

A tragedy

It is a fact, according to all contemporary observers, that whole continents—especially South-East Asia and the Far East, Africa, South America and Central America—are in a state of profound inequality when compared with the favoured nations, particularly North America and Europe.

As things are now, this inequality is seen on the *economic* level in the horrors of undernourishment (two men out of three suffer from hunger), in the underexploitation of local resources, and in under-employment. It can be seen on the social, cultural and medical levels in illiteracy (one out of every two adults cannot read), in inadequate administrative and political structures, in inadequate housing conditions, in the results of uncontrolled fertility, in failings in the quantity and quality of education, in the inferior status of women, in the prevalence of sickness and excessive infantile mortality rates, etc.

Looking into the future, one can see that this inequality will take on more dramatic proportions still if energetic measures are not taken now. If things are allowed to go on as they are, the difference between the standards of living of the rich nations and those of the poor ones will have doubled by the year 2000, when, according to the latest demographic forecasts, there will be about five thousand million people on the earth. Since, in general, the birth rate is at present much higher in undernourished countries than in others, the problem of underdevelopment is closely bound up with the demographic problem.

A threat to peace

This state of things is the more tragic in that it is a permanent source of international disputes. It has provoked, and unless the ills are cured it will provoke again, violent reactions of the "have-nots" against the "haves". This, as Pius XII implied in an address to the Food and Agriculture Organization of the United Nations, constitutes a constant threat to the peace of the world:

> Nations favoured by nature or the progress of civilization will have a harsh awakening one day if they do not now strive to ensure that the less favoured nations also develop and live in a manner worthy of man. To awaken a sense of collective responsibility in a great number of peoples and nations is a high and noble task, especially if it produces enlightened and generous action. In these days of suspicion, division and revolution, the moral effect of such a result would be even more important than its material consequences.

The common good requires that in each economic unit, and in the greater economic unit that is the whole world, the conditions of its achievement should be realized. The common good of mankind implies that through the efforts of all and the best use of all resources, the distribution of the results of that effort should create mutual trust and peace among the nations. Such trust and peace, which are essential elements of the good of mankind, cannot be achieved now, if the disparities between the standards of living of rich and poor nations, which are already too great, continue to increase. Pope John XXIII has recently stressed this point: "The nations of the world are becoming more and more dependent on one another, but even so, it will not be possible to preserve a lasting peace so long as these glaring economic and social inequalities persist" (*Mater et magistra*, § 157).

Organizations for international aid

The growing awareness of the problem has produced the beginnings of action to cope with it. The unsatisfied needs of the poorer nations and the danger to peace which they involve have in fact given birth during the last fifteen years to two kinds of organization: specialized inter-governmental agencies associated with U.N.O., such as the F.A.O., W.H.O., and U.N.E.S.C.O.; and fiscal organizations such as the International Bank for Reconstruction and Development, intended to promote and finance international aid.[2] The same growing awareness of the problem has also produced various governmental organizations and actions for bilateral aid in a number of nations, and numerous public, semi-public and private organizations developed to train the necessary experts for technical cooperation and the research scientists who make it possible and determine its nature.

THE JUDGEMENTS OF INTERNATIONAL MORALITY ON THE GENERAL SITUATION

Catholic international moralists can only rejoice that there has been this awareness of the problem and that a start has

---

[2] We cannot here analyse in detail the structure and activity of these specialized agencies; see Bibliography for sources of further information.

been made towards dealing with it. Pope John XXIII has recently said as much:

> International and regional organizations, national and private societies, all are working towards this goal, increasing day by day the measure of their own technical cooperation in all productive spheres. By their combined efforts thousands of young people are being given facilities for attending the universities of more advanced countries, and acquiring an up-to-date scientific, technical and professional training. World banking institutes, single States and private persons are helping to furnish the capital for an ever richer network of economic enterprises in these underdeveloped countries. . . . It is therefore a source of great joy to us to see those nations which enjoy a high degree of economic wealth helping the underdeveloped nations to raise their own standard of living (*Mater et magistra*, §§ 165, 160).

However, this general approval is accompanied by certain recommendations, in order that tomorrow may be better than today. These recommendations may be summed up in the following rules.

First rule: The hierarchy of values must be respected.

The Catholic moralist cannot regard the realities of underdevelopment, and, consequently, of the aids to development provided by the more highly developed nations, as existing only on the material and economic level. In fact, a true policy of aid towards development should set up as an ideal for all men the whole good of man, on all levels—material economic, social, cultural, spiritual and religious. No development plan, for a Christian moralist, can be really firmly based and fruitful unless it takes account of the wholeness and the oneness of the good of man and the hierarchy of values thus implied. What is to be developed is man— what is human in man, and also, because of man's supernatural vocation, what is divine in man. To enable man to become all that he ought to be, having regard to all that he is: that is the aim.

Second rule: Human spontaneity must be respected.

The development of a nation ought above all to move towards making a people sufficiently mature to supply its own needs. Forms of aid which are educative and constructive are therefore to be preferred to pure assistance. It therefore follows that priority should be given to the formation of men, not only from the point of view of professional and technical skills, but culturally and socially. Then there follow in order of importance the material infrastructures and economic equipment.

In his encyclical *Mater et magistra*, Pope John XXIII suggests that organizations for aid towards development should imitate in their own spheres the action of the Church in hers: "Moreover, in becoming, as it were, the life-blood of these people, the Church is not, nor does she consider herself to be, a foreign body in their midst. Her presence brings about the rebirth, the resurrection, of each individual in Christ; and the man who is reborn and rises again in Christ never feels himself constrained from without. He feels himself free in the very depth of his being " (§ 180). In concrete terms, this means the preparation, by means of the aid provided, of native experts capable of assuming responsibility in matters professional, administrative, technical, legal, political, etc.

Third rule: Man's originality must be respected

In Chapter IV we stated, following the teachings of Pius XII, that the unity of man's nature did not imply a uniformity of individuals or of nations. Each case of underdevelopment must therefore be studied in itself and for itself, as it is, since each man, and each community of men, is "the most irreplaceable of beings."

Mater et magistra explicitly makes this requirement. Pope John says that the more advanced communities must as far as possible respect the individuality of each nation, for they "have certain unmistakable characteristics of their own, resulting from the nature of the particular region and its inhabitants, with their time-honoured traditions and customs. . . . They must beware of making the assistance they give an excuse for forcing these people into their own national mould" (§§ 169–170).

Fourth rule: Aid must be offered in a disinterested way and with a spirit of service.

All intervention for the benefit of countries on the road to development must be inspired by the spirit of service, with no ulterior motives of prestige or national advantage. *Mater et magistra* firmly calls the spirit of domination which could thus insinuate itself into this field "a new form of colonialism":

> There is also a further temptation which the economically developed nations must resist: that of giving technical and financial aid with a view to gaining control over the political situation in the underdeveloped countries, and furthering their own plans for world domination.
> Let us be quite clear on this point. A nation that acted from these motives would in fact be introducing a new form of colonialism—cleverly disguised, no doubt, but in no respect less blameworthy than that from which many nations have recently emerged. Such action would, moreover, have a disastrous effect on international relations, and constitute a menace to world peace.
> Necessity, therefore, and justice demand that all such technical and financial aid be given in a sincere spirit of political disinterestedness. It must be given for the sole purpose of helping the underdeveloped nations to achieve their own economic and social growth.

If this can be achieved, then a precious contribution will have been made to the formation of a world community, in which each individual nation, conscious of its rights and duties, can work on terms of equality with the rest for the attainment of universal prosperity (§§ 171–174).

So the lack of capital and economic infrastructures in certain countries should lead to offers from richer countries of totally disinterested investment.

Fifth rule: The present level of international aid must be raised.

If the richer nations of the world have begun to be aware of their responsibilities towards the underdeveloped countries, it must nevertheless be admitted that their efforts so far have been insufficient. To take but one example, the total of the contributions made by the western powers to underdeveloped countries and to multilateral organizations between 1956 and 1959 was only just over twenty-eight thousand million dollars. Moreover, the agencies responsible for development lack not only money but men. Experts capable of drawing up an economic development plan adapted to the special needs of any given African or Asian country are still extremely few and far between, and so are qualified specialists in tropical agriculture. There is also a great lack of teachers, doctors and administrators who are willing to serve African or Asian governments through national organizations for technical assistance. Besides this, the parallel efforts of the different organizations for development aid are insufficiently coordinated.

In view of such lacks as these, we can understand the words of John XXIII in *Mater et magistra*: "It is a magnificent work that they are doing. . . . It is a work, however, which needs to be increased, and we hope that the years ahead will see the wealthier nations making even greater efforts for the scientific, technical and economic advancement of those political communities whose development is still only in its initial stages" (§ 165).

SOME DOCTRINAL OBSERVATIONS

To these rules, derived from the "historico-prudential" judgements of the situation as it was in 1961, when the Pope wrote, the Catholic moralist must add some doctrinal observations on the exact nature of the duty to aid less favoured nations, on the "subjects" of that duty, on some of the stumbling-blocks which may cause such aid to go astray, and on the ways in which it should be undertaken if it is to be fully effective.

The exact nature of the duty

What are the real bases of this duty to help other nations? How far does it extend? How compelling is it? To these questions the Catholic moralist must try to give the answers.

First of all, he sees in this duty an obligation grounded in the *natural solidarity of mankind*. Pope John has said in his encyclical *Ad Petri cathedram*: "God did not create men as enemies but as brothers. He gave them the earth to cultivate by their labour so that all might enjoy its fruits and draw from it all they need for their nourishment and their wants." And later he added: "To this first reason—the natural community of man—can be added the requirements of the universal common good. It is not only persons who are drawn together in the unity of human kind, but also the communities which make up mankind. The different nations are only communities of men, that is, of brothers, who ought to aim, in fraternal unity, not only for the proper end of each but for the common good of all mankind." The Pope also spoke of this duty based on humanity in *Mater et magistra* (§ 161).

But this natural obligation is also based on *supernatural charity*, which must, as we have said in Chapter IV, unite all men, in all fields of human relations, in the Mystical Body of Christ.

Yet is is not enough to reduce this duty to help underdeveloped countries simply to a matter of charitable assistance. As John XXIII has said (*Mater et magistra*, § 161), it is also a matter of *justice*.

It is in fact part of the order of nature, created by God, that the total of the good things existing in the world should benefit all men; such was the teaching of the great Doctors of the Middle Ages, and this principle of the common destination of the goods of the earth has been formally stated by recent papal pronouncements.

Besides, traditional Catholic morality has frequently had to face analogous paradoxical situations within some given national community: certain individuals had more goods than they needed for their existence or well-being, while others lacked the means to meet the normal necessities of life and lived in wretchedness. Faced with such situations, traditional Catholic morality required that in such circumstances, *in the name of justice*, the superfluity of the former should serve to relieve the misery of the others, so far as the goods in question could be shared.

This principle, which governs the relations between individuals within a national community, should be extended to cover the relations between nations within the international community. It is expressed in *duties* imposed by justice on the rich nations with regard to poorer countries, and also, reciprocally, in *rights* possessed by nations suffering from want with regard to more generously endowed nations. In other words, the existence of a real world community embracing all mankind establishes a system of rights and duties, on the level of justice, properly so called, which should govern all relations within one global society which aims at realizing one good common to all its members.

On whom does social justice impose these duties?

In a general and diffuse way they are imposed, first, on *all men*. So each man has the duty and the right to initiate the relevant private action for his own part.

But because of the insufficiency of such private actions and of the means at their disposal, *each State* has the duty, and at the same time the right, to contribute towards the realization of the development of peoples in need. This intervention of one State in favour of another is justified in the same way as that of one individual in favour of another. Nevertheless, if any government should impose on its own nationals burdens such as taxes for the benefit of some foreign nation or nations, it should always remember that it is first and foremost responsible for the common good and the rule of social justice within the nation of which it is the politico-juridical organ.

But these duties, based on social justice, also concern any *international organization*, which can therefore *demand*, in the name of the common good of mankind, which is its responsibility, an appropriate contribution from each of its members. This is explicitly recognized in the United Nations Charter, which requires all its member-States "to promote higher standards of living, full employment, and conditions of economic and social progress and development" in wider conditions of freedom (Art. 55). In a more detailed manner, Article 25 of the Universal Declaration of Human Rights states that "everyone has the right to a standard of living adequate for the health and well-being of himself and of his family, including food, clothing, housing, medical care and necessary social services, and the right to security in the event of unemployment, sickness, disability, widowhood, old age or other lack of livelihood in circumstances beyond his control". It is for these reasons that the United Nations has created, as we have said, its specialized agencies.

Two points may be added:

1. These rights and duties of the international organization are not substitutes for the rights and duties of each of its member-States. There is therefore scope for inquiry, in each case, so as to discover the most efficient method and the one corresponding most closely with the nature of aid between nations. It may be that historical circumstances or particular opportunities put this or that nation in a specially good position to help some other particular people or State. But to look at the problem in the abstract, at least, international aid will perhaps seem sometimes more disinterested if it has a collective appearance and does not seem to come from a single country.

2. Pius XII returned several times to the idea that Europe had a particularly serious commitment in this matter of development aid, because of all that she had received in the past from the countries once under her care, and the responsibility for them she had thus assumed.

> Europe knows, as the whole world knows, that all men are brothers, and that they are all called to work to lessen the miseries of all mankind, to eradicate the scandals of famine and ignorance (November 4th, 1957).

> It seems to us essential that Europe retain in Africa the ability to use her educative and formative influence, and that she should support that influence with generous and comprehensive material aid to help raise the standard of living of the peoples of Africa and to use to the full the rich natural resources of the continent (June 13th, 1957).

> We do indeed rejoice to see more exchanges between Europe and Africa, linked as they are by so many historical and geographical ties. There is in the common exploitation of the considerable riches which the Creator has planted in the soil and under the soil of the African continent, a much more effective coming together than any protestations of friendship. Working together has always been a providential way of

getting to know and respect one another. If immediate diver-
gences of interests can give rise to temporary disputes, a reasonable care for the common good, a lofty vision inspired by
far-sighted prudence, and feelings of mutual confidence will
lead to a search for true agreement in which the rights and
aspirations of each will be respected (April 12th, 1958).

Some impossible ways

If development aid is to arrive at results which are morally
sound, according to Catholic morality, then it cannot be
given in certain ways, which are bound to be futile. The most
harmful of these ways, as it seems to Catholicism, are these:

1. That of *liberal paternalism*, which will end, beginning
with technical assistance, by becoming a more or less dis-
guised economic neo-colonialism.

2. That of *Marxism*, which can only achieve some
material development at the expense of a total violation of
personality and of natural communities, especially that of
the family.

3. That of *vague nationalism*, which leads recently
liberated nations, still underdeveloped, to refuse to work
along with the international cooperative activities necessary
to their own development. Pope John XXIII said in an
address to a meeting of African cultural leaders on April 1st,
1959: "It is to be hoped that offers of aid made in a spirit
of disinterested service and not with the expectation of
selfish profit will be received with feelings worthy of
generous hearts, free from the narrowness of an inflamed
nationalism."

4. That of *rivalry in spheres of influence*: the development
of underdeveloped countries must not become the battlefield of the two opposed blocs of East and West. Nor must
it simply provide opportunities for each to outbid the other,
which would do as much harm to those who thus became
guilty of conscious or unconscious imperialism as to those

thus aided, who would be treated as means only, and not as the ends of the action taken.

5. Any ways which *contravene the laws of life* (see *Mater et magistra* on "Population increase and economic development"). Some believe that birth control is the only adequate remedy for the problems of world over-population and those caused by the high birth-rate in certain of the underdeveloped countries. Now Catholicism is adamant in its rejection of the use of contraceptives. Not that the Church, contrary to what so many non-Catholics wrongly imagine, denies that there is a case for family limitation in over-populated countries. The Church is not in favour of an unrestrained and ever higher birth-rate left entirely to the caprices of men's instincts. Pius XII himself used the phrase "family limitation" and said that the Church by no means advocated that the birth-rate should be allowed thoughtlessly and irrationally to run wild. But if the Church refuses to permit the use of pharmaceutical and mechanical methods of contraception to produce the limitation of family size which is necessary in over-populated countries, that refusal is only the logical answer to the many questions she asks because of her unyielding care and respect for man, the whole man.

The sexual act of human beings cannot be thought of as the simple brute fact of animal instinct: it should surely express in an objective fashion all the subtle beauties of the love of husband and wife. The deliberate frustration of the act must imperil the inner rightness of those relations of love. A policy involving the use of contraceptives, under the pretext of effectively and quickly curing the nutritional problems of an over-populated country, must cause in that society of human beings a serious underdevelopment of the spiritual bases of the physical relations between the sexes. Such a policy would be like trying to cure the plague by infecting people with cholera: it is to cure famine with a perversion, to want to abolish the anomalies of hunger by introducing sexual aberrations.

It is true that such ethical judgements will not make it easy to find immediate and adequate measures to solve the tragic problems of over-population now facing the world. They might even be held to jeopardize development schemes already begun in various parts of the globe. But in reality, they prevent policies of development from being degraded; they save technical aid offered to over-populated nations from the danger of slipping gradually into the monstrous forms of what is simply veterinary intervention, attempting by no matter what means to regulate in this or that country, in proportion to the availability of food, the reproduction of the local stock of mammalian bipeds.

It is at once obvious, *a fortiori*, that Catholic morality must reject as immoral any recourse to *abortion*, since from the standpoint of Catholic doctrine, abortion is practically equivalent to murder.[3]

Some ways which are possible

Faced with the problems of over-population, the Catholic moralist urges the nations to look for solutions in three directions:

1. A concerted worldwide effort to develop further the resources of the globe and to improve their distribution; this implies first a reduction of the amount spent on armaments.

2. Worldwide collaboration permitting and encouraging the coordinated and fruitful exchange of knowledge, capital and men; this implies some rational improvement in present policies concerning emigration and immigration.

[3] On birth control and abortion, see S. de Lestapis, *Family Planning and Modern Problems: a Catholic Analysis*, trans. from the 2nd revised edn by Reginald H. Trevett (Herder and Burns & Oates, 1961).

3. Some "family limitation", but by methods conforming with the principles expressed by Pius XII and allowed by natural morality and the Church (sexual self-control and the use of the "safe period").

Such, in broad outline, are the principles which should govern all relations of international aid, according to the Christian moralist. It remains now, to conclude our survey of international morality, to examine how and why the Catholic Church tries to ensure the rule of international morality in the world. This will be the subject of the next and last chapter.

CHAPTER IX

THE CHURCH AND THE RULE OF INTERNATIONAL MORALITY IN THE WORLD

In the foregoing chapters we have given a summary of certain conditions which are necessary, according to Catholic international morality, for the rule of international morality in the world. First, all nations must order all their activity with a view to the common good of the world, as the supreme political value. For this to be possible, those who govern must adopt a spirit of true charity. Second, there must be established, preserved and continually improved, according to the historical situation, an international organization which is able to assume effective responsibility for that common good of the world. Third, the rulers of the nations must strive to substitute for the settlement of international disputes by war, settlements which are peaceful and juridical. Fourth, they must institute and administer such international aid as shall, progressively, but as swiftly and as completely as possible, abolish disparities in the standards of living of different nations and shall assure for all their full development. And last, there must be in Europe, thanks to the more and more stable building up of European institutions, an end to the old historical antagonisms which have caused so many wars in the past.

But, according to the Catholic moralist, there is yet one more supreme condition to be stated: the Catholic Church, without becoming confused with the world political authority, and without going outside her own field, which is not that of political, technical or temporal affairs properly speaking, but that of spiritual values, must fulfil her mission of educating the minds of men, of guarding natural and supernatural values, and of forming rightly men's wills.

The affirmation of this principle was as it were a single theme running through all the Christmas messages of Pius XII. It is easily explained, in various ways, and we can do it by bringing together certain propositions scattered in the foregoing pages.

1. We have shown above that a world political authority can only be living, truly established and truly recognized if all the men who run it and all the nations that it governs are agreed on the system of human values which are to be pursued in the lives and history of men. Now the Church knows and proclaims and intends herself to be, in the name of Jesus Christ who is God, the one true depository and guardian of absolute and universal values.

To be more precise, the system of fundamental values at the basis of international order is, as suggested in Chapter I, both a system of natural values and one of properly supernatural values, the former, because of the freely given but commanding Design of God, being subordinated to the latter. Now, because of original sin and its consequences, mankind, in virtue of his natural condition itself, cannot recognize "easily, with certitude and without risk of error" (Vatican Council, 1870) even the natural values which are essentially, and despite man's sin, on the same level as his reason. Moreover—and above all—the reason, left to itself without the help of the Revelation in Christ, is utterly incapable of discerning the properly supernatural ends and values to which mankind is called by God, in a manner at once free and compelling, freely to order all its efforts, on the international level as on all other levels of natural and temporal life and action. So it is by virtue of a double title, natural and supernatural, that the value-judgements provided by the teaching of the Church are spiritually indispensable to the community of nations.

2. We have also shown that the spiritual formation of the minds of men and the spiritual education of their wills is as pressingly urgent as the progressive establishment of a world political authority endowed with effective power—legislative, executive, judiciary and penal. Now the Church knows and proclaims and intends herself to be, because of a specific command from Jesus Christ who is God, the one true former of men's minds and the one true educator of their wills. She knows that she alone is able, and that she alone has the right and the duty, to save mankind from the ignorance and the inner servitude natural to sinful man.

3. Again, we have established that a worldwide policy for a community of man cannot be defined in terms of the "letter of the law" only, of a positive body of public international law built up and continually changing to cope with unforeseeable historical situations; such a law is bound to be "dated" and therefore inevitably relative and transitory. Such a policy needs a *spirit*, to make possible the permanent discovery of the principles underlying the temporary structures of the various codes of law required by the unforeseen movement of history. Now the mission of the Church is essentially a spiritual mission: her rôle is to kindle and to maintain in the hearts of men the flame of the very Spirit of God, by appealing to principles and to her "historico-prudential" judgements; it is to provide a perpetual *recta sapere* for those who have the responsibility of finding the road to be followed by mankind, when that

road is not completely determined beforehand by the juridical decisions already established and codified.

4. One more remark must, however, be made: we must make quite plain the need for the Church to be able to play her own part, alongside that of the political community of the nations organized by the nations for the nations. Even supposing that at any given time the institutional structures and the codifications of public international law do give adequate expression to the order of *natural and temporal* values which fall directly within their province, they still cannot on their own and simply for that reason enable men to follow effectively that *supernatural* vocation which God calls mankind, freely yet compellingly, to realize. Such secular institutional structures and such codifications of law, however well-adapted they may be in human terms, yet possess, as do all things human and all things natural, a certain ambivalence with regard to the supernatural end of man. As such, they are of course in practice "Christianizable" and "Christianizing"; but they are also potentially "Satanizable" and "Satanizing". So the advanced development (in human terms) of a country may actually end, in practice, by making it possible for its citizens to shut themselves in, in what is human only, so as to worship material comforts idolatrously, as if comfort were the supreme value in life. *Mater et magistra* reminds contemporary nations that are economically developed of this ambivalence: "Scientific and technical progress, economic development and the betterment of living conditions, are certainly valuable elements in a civilization. But we must realize that they are essentially instrumental in character. They are not supreme values in themselves" (§ 175).

So, with regard to the international community, whatever its degree of rational organization, the same vital question must always be asked: What is its spirit? Is it that of

Lucifer, claiming to enable man to be self-sufficient so as to perfect himself, making a god without God and against God? Or is it that of Christ, desiring to make man more able to become "god" in God through Christ? In other words, is the fundamental inspiration of the political organization of the nations that of a worldwide, atheist humanism, or that of a worldwide humanism infused with the spirit of the Gospel?

For all these reasons, the Church cannot remain outside the movements of international life now occurring in the world. But politicians must not misunderstand this intention and effort of the Church. The Catholic hierarchy no more dream of exercising any supreme political power or civil jurisdiction over an international organization than they do of exercising such powers over any State. It would thus be quite wrong to interpret the desires of the Church as the claim of the "Vatican" to lord it politically over "secular" powers, telling them in technical terms precisely how to behave internationally. What the Church wants above all is to keep the minds of men—and especially those of the men directly responsible for international affairs—aware of the meaning of man, of the meaning of what is human in man and of what is divine in him. For the Church believes that only if it is completely inspired by the spirit of Jesus Christ can international politics be truly good for mankind.

It is fair, then, to ask how the Church is going to provide the nations and international organizations with this spiritual inspiration without setting up a kind of ecclesiastical overlordship. The history of recent times shows that the Church can do it in two ways.

1. First, the bishops, and the pope at their head, can often intervene by publishing doctrinal statements. Such, for example, was *Mater et magistra*. Sometimes they will do this to remind men of the values to be kept in mind in the situations which arise, and to publish some wise and prudent

counsel. Generally, they will leave to those who are experts in the field of international affairs the technical analysis of situations which give rise, or may give rise, to problems, and the technical choice of the political means to be used to reach a morally sound solution. But sometimes the hierarchy will still speak out, when certain actions have already been undertaken by certain States or by international authority, if it appears to them that the means adopted ignore or even go against certain values; but then it will be to point out the error concerning those values. Sometimes, if the political measures taken do seem to be in accord with the rules of morality, the hierarchy will again raise its voice, either to disarm the unjustified criticisms of false "moralists" with mistaken ideas, or to emphasize by their approval the rules which ought to be respected and are being respected in the case in question. Lastly, as did John XXIII in *Mater et magistra*, the hierarchy may formulate some general principles as being more or less urgently in need of being stated.

If we add that, within the general field of a common spiritual orthodoxy on the matter of values, Catholicism nevertheless often leaves room, because of the uncertainties of the situation or the means available, for several different but legitimate political alternatives, we can see how the exercise of the Church's *magisterium* (whether or not it is in practice supported by canonical measures depending on the jurisdiction in matters of religion which the hierarchy possesses, even in relation to temporal actions) cannot be confused with the exercise of any civil jurisdiction or with a political overlordship of the Church in international affairs.

2. But of course, strictly speaking, the Church is not simply the hierarchy: as Pius XII said, "the laity is also the Church". To see that international politics is permeated by the spirit of Christ, the Church relies on the laity, on the world of her baptized children. Some she asks to serve in

private, secular international organizations or, specifically, in Catholic ones. Others she expects to take whatever part their own abilities make possible in the specialist work of international organizations of the official kind, at all levels. Here again, it is important not to be deceived: in suggesting to certain Catholic laymen that they might take on this or that official position, the hierarchy is not asking them to take part in the work of an official international organization *as Catholics*, in order to work for the Church's political control of such organizations. Such Catholics would be much mistaken if they expected to receive from the hierarchy orders and instructions of a technical nature concerning their professional functions.

In fact, the Church only desires that within those international organizations they act and work *in a Catholic manner*, that is, in the spirit of the Gospel, in the spirit of the last pages of *Mater et magistra*.

So the Church counts on them, but not so as to make the temporal international power serve her own interests or to absorb it into herself; she wishes to provide through them, to a large extent, the "soul" which is necessary to the organized body politic of the world if it is to be and remain a living body. She hopes that thus international affairs will be wholly directed towards that "supreme spiritual value" of which Pope John XXIII has spoken, the pursuit of which alone can ensure the safety of the world, namely, the supernatural and divine virtue of Charity.

SELECT BIBLIOGRAPHY

In this series: HODGSON, P.: *Nuclear Physics in Peace and War*; HOLLIS, Christopher: *The Church and Economics* (American edn, *Christianity and Economics*); RÉTIF, André, S.J.: *The Catholic Spirit.*

AQUINAS, St Thomas: *Summa Theologica*, translated by Fathers of the English Dominican Province, London, Burns and Oates, and New York, Benziger, 1957.

AUGUSTINE, St: *City of God*, two volumes, London, Dent, and New York, Dutton, 1939.

BIRKENHEAD, Earl of: *International Law*, 6th edn by R. Moelwyn-Hughes, London, Dent, 1927.

BISHOP, William W., Jr.: *International Law, Cases and Materials*, New York, Prentice-Hall.

BRIERLY, J. L.: *The Law of Nations*, London and New York, 1955.

BRUEHL, Charles D.: *The Pope's Plan for Social Reconstruction*, New York, Adair, 1949.

DAWSON, Christopher: *Religion and the Modern State*, London and New York, Sheed and Ward, 1938.

FENWICK, Charles G.: *International Law*, New York, Appleton.

FREMANTLE, Anne: *The Papal Encyclicals in their Historical Context*, New York, New American Library of World Literature, 1956.

GUERRY, E.: *The Social Teaching of the Church*, London, St Paul Publications, 1961.

GURIAN, W., and FITZSIMMONS, M. A.: *The Catholic Church and World Affairs*, Oxford, Blackwell, and Notre Dame, Ind., Univ. of Notre Dame Press, 1954.

HALES, E. E. Y.: *The Catholic Church in the Modern World*, London, Eyre and Spottiswoode, 1958.

HARTMANN, F. H. (Editor): *Basic Documents of International Relations*, New York, McGraw, 1951.

HUGHES, Philip: *The Popes' New Order: A Systematic Study of the Social Encyclicals and Addresses from Leo XIII to Pius XII*, London, Burns and Oates, 1943.

LESTAPIS, S. de, S.J.: *Family Planning and Modern Problems*, London, Burns and Oates, and New York, Herder, 1961.

MARITAIN, Jacques: *Man and the State* (ed. by R. O'Sullivan, Q.C.), London, Hollis and Carter, 1954, and Chicago, Univ. of Chicago Press, 1955; *The Twilight of Civilization*, translated by L. Landry, London and New York, Sheed and Ward, 1946.

POUND, R.: *Law and Morals*, Chapel Hill, N.C., Univ. of N. Carolina Press, and London, Oxford Univ. Press, 1926.

REUTER, P.: *International Institutions*, translated by J. M. Chapman, London, George Allen and Unwin, 1958.

RYAN, J. A., and BOLAND, F. F.: *Catholic Principles of Politics*, New York, Macmillan.

SOHN, L. B. (Editor): *Basic Documents of the United Nations*, London, Stevens, 1956.

STRATMAN, F.: *War and Christianity Today*, London, Blackfriars, 1957, and Westminster, Md., Newman Press, 1058.

VERONESE, V. (Editor): *World Crisis and the Catholic: Studies published on the occasion of the second World Congress for the Lay Apostolate*, London and New York, Sheed and Ward, 1958.

WILLIAMS, M. J.: *Catholic Social Thought*, New York, Ronald Press, 1954.

Texts and translations of Suarez and Vitoria have been published in the series *Classics of International Law*, Washington, 1944 and 1947.